Sister Mary Ambrosine

Evenings At School

or, Dramas for my girls 1883

Sister Mary Ambrosine

Evenings At School
or, Dramas for my girls 1883

ISBN/EAN: 9783741185120

Manufactured in Europe, USA, Canada, Australia, Japa

Cover: Foto ©Andreas Hilbeck / pixelio.de

Manufactured and distributed by brebook publishing software (www.brebook.com)

Sister Mary Ambrosine

Evenings At School

EVENINGS AT SCHOOL;

OR,

DRAMAS FOR MY GIRLS.

BY

NEW YORK:
D. APPLETON AND COMPANY,
1, 3, AND 5 BOND STREET.
1883.

PREFACE.

These dramas, hastily penned as required, have grown from the duties of one, a guardian and instructress of girlhood for many years. Their performance has occasionally enlivened the evenings of the school term; and they have served when it has been difficult to provide selections unexceptionable in tone and adapted exclusively to female character.

The favorable acceptance of a previous little work of the kind has induced this publication. It is offered with peculiar regard to those who labor in a like vocation—one which the writer has loved to believe implied in the Divine injunction, "Consider the *lilies* of the *field*, how they grow."

THE AUTHORESS.

New York, *May* 16, 1883.

CONTENTS.

	PAGE
THE VOYAGE OF LIFE	9
THE CROWN OF GLORY	31
THE ENCHANTED ISLE	61
THE MUSIC OF A MORNING DREAM	75
THE VESTALS	91
LITTLE TIPTOE	145

THE VOYAGE OF LIFE.

ALLEGORICAL MELODRAMA.

"Lead me in the eternal way."—PSALMS.

CHARACTERS.

YOUTH.
SCIENCE.
FAITH.
HOPE.
CHARITY.
HUMILITY. } VIRTUES.
PURITY.
ZEAL.
PRIDE.
SLOTH. } VICES.
PLEASURE.

A CHORUS OF INVISIBLE ANGELS.

THE VOYAGE OF LIFE.

PROLOGUE.

L<small>IFE</small>'s sea, o'erhung with warring gloom and light.
    Fair Youth embarking its veiled reefs, above :
Launched from the misty shores of Boundless Might,
    To port in radiant realms of endless love.
Ah, sea of perils !—rock, and shoal, and calm.
    The Soul untried—her fragile barque of clay.
Faith takes the helm, clear-eyed, and strong of arm ;
    Bright Hope the prow, with many a glorious ray
Wreathing her forehead, and the timid Soul,
    Supported on the heart of Charity,
Sees, in the distance, cloudy gates uproll—
    Fair angel hands, that beckon lovingly.
Tossed on the billowy tide, the little craft
    Sweeps on ; with winds of grace her sails to swell,
Nor sees the waterspout eject, abaft,
    The Shadowy Vices from the tombs of hell.
They board, they charm. The Virtues fair take wing.
    The Passions taking helm, to whirlpools nigh ;
But lo ! bright cherubs, zealous for their king,

Swift, to the succor of the sad Soul, fly.
They threaten, counsel, scourge, defend, and plead,
To triumph. May ye all the lesson heed!
If faultless, persevere; if frail, the strife
Renew yet once again, O Voyagers of Life!

THE VOYAGE OF LIFE.

Faith enters, conducting Youth.

FAITH.

Hitherto, O timid child of earth!
I have impelled, with sure but gentle hand,
Thy barque upon a laughing, shallow stream,
Girding with silvery zone, this sheltered dale.
Here clustering foliage, hanging to the sun,
Its ripening wealth of richly tinted pomes,
Bordered the margin, then again it wound
Through gardens, where the inconstant zephyr hung
O'er the fair flowers, enamored of their grace.
The soft, illusive lights of early dawn
Have lain around thy shallop's airy keel;
And home-affection's enervating air
Hath tempered the more healthful mountain breeze.
Lo! the scene widens to a changeful sea,
Now wild with tempest, then as lucid, calm,
As inland lake, in some soft southern clime.
Borne in these arms, which have thy cradle been

Since infancy, thou canst not dare its moods.
Lo! Reason's sunrise—yea, and Science calls.

YOUTH.

"Science!" Who is she, Faith?

FAITH.

A teacher, Youth,
And mine half-sister. She approaches—see!
Her glimmering taper, and her opening scroll.
She'll bear thee on, through star-lit halls of space;
And teach thine ear to interpret the grand psalm,
That th' spheres sing unto Omnipotence.
She'll traverse Air and Earth with thee—will lead
Down into rayless subterranean depths.
Still, as thou onward journeyest, will she turn,
With hand uplifted, saying, reverently:
"Listen!" and thou shalt hear, and shrink to hear,
The Eternal Artist whisper nigh, "*I Am!*"
Oft will she send thee unto me, to learn,
As to a wiser mistress; for I taught,
Ere she was born, that which to-day I teach,
Holding to earth, the gates of Heaven, ajar.
Yea, ever, as thou goest, she, in detail,
Will prove, by reason and research, the truths
Which I proclaim, bidding mankind receive
On mine assertion.

YOUTH *to* SCIENCE.

I will follow thee.

SCIENCE.

But watch thou warily, for Satan oft
Assumes my garb and place.

YOUTH.

How should I know?

SCIENCE.

He still, insidiously, will inculcate
First doubt of Faith, rebellion then, and scorn.
Faith's torch extinguished, Conscience casts aside
Hers, and the Soul is darkened, utterly.
The Virtues flee it, leaving open wide
Its portal to the birds and bats of night.

FAITH.

Onward, O Youth! Take thou the helm and still
Follow my torch, though its unwavering light
Should guide where storms in wildest fury boil;
And Death the darkness haunt, athirst for prey.
Beloved of Jesus, do not shrink appalled;
For I will summon, to attend thy way,
Celestial Sisters, from the love-lit halls
Of ever-youthful joy—thy journey's goal.

YOUTH.

Who can, unawed, look forth on such a scene?
Lo! to the left the rippling waves lie smooth,
As tho' the sea nymphs, dancing there, had passed,
Scattering from urns of amber and of pearl,
Unnumbered rubies o'er their glistening path.

And yet the beauty of that restful calm
Thou biddest me distrust ; and warnest me
That it but lulls the mariner to sleep,
To backward bear his barque, league after league,

With movement swift but imperceptible :
Till he, from lethargy upstarting, wakes

To find himself a helpless, hopeless waif,
Tossed by relentless tides upon the shores
Of endless bondage and supine despair;
Marking, in distance vanishing, the forms
Of Time and Opportunity, far flown.
Thou wouldst that I should dare yon wrathful waste
Of wrestling waters, crested o'er with foam,
Shadowed with wind-torn clouds, through which escape
A few stray beams obliquely thrown to light
The possibilities of dangers nigh.
Safer, perhaps, yet, O unerring friend !
Mark how the scornful tide casts to the sands
Wreck after wreck, nor wonder that I fear.
Ah ! if thou canst not, unassisted, guide
My shallop to its haven, call, dear Faith,
Thy sister Virtues. Bid them all attend.

FAITH (*summons* CHARITY).

Come from the Heart of Christ,
   O Charity Divine !
Come, with thy thurible, whose odors are
The sighs of sanctity, exiled afar
   From that fond Home of thine.

Come, with thy smile serene.
   Thy ever upturned brow,
Marked with the impress of communings high.
Come, that to God we live—to idols die.
   Thy place shall be the prow.

(*Summoning* HOPE.)

Love, on the Cross, consumed,
　　Makes it a sacred pyre.
Spring from it, buoyant Hope, all phœnix-like,
And, when the tempest lowers, sweetly strike
　　The chords of thy clear lyre.

Sing of that Land, in which,
　　Unto the spirit's vase,
Love's torrents, in such mighty volume, sweep,
That, did not Hands Divine the chalice keep,
　　'Twould shatter, to the base.

From a chorus of unseen angels, as CHARITY *and* HOPE *advance, a voice sings the following solo:*

O ye angelic hosts! all love and purity,
　　Ye living lyres, swept by the Spirit's Wing,
Shake Paradise with songs of jubilee.
　　The power and mercy of the Father sing—
　　Sanctus! Sanctus! Sanctus! Jehovah—King.

CHORUS.

Amen! Amen! His bounteous Hand hath given
　　Earth's mines, their gems, her fields, their golden sheaves.
Seas yield their prey, and bless the winds of heaven.
　　The vintage laughs, amid thick clustering leaves.
　　Yet greater gifts, unthanked, the Spirit breathes.

FAITH (*summoning* HUMILITY).

Come, from the Virgin's heart,
  O Truth—Humility!
With meek retreating eye, and reverent brow—
Strong in the might of peace and patience, thou,
  Our strength and armor be.

Come, in unstudied grace,
  Unto thy calm heart pressed,
Aromad violets, a beauteous wreath,
Cerulean, as heavenly thoughts beneath,
  Give to us truth and rest.

(*Summoning* PURITY.)

Bring, from the Throne of thrones,
  Robed in ethereal light,
Fair Purity, O "Living Creatures"—ye
Who "Holy! Holy!" cry, unceasingly:
  Resting not "day or night."

Poor fallen Earth will deck
  In vestal snow, untrod,
To greet the seraph, and her infants fair
With late-blown lilies in their clustering hair
  Shall ask to look on God.*

ANGELIC SOLO.

"O ye angelic hosts!" etc.

---

* "Blessed are the clean of heart: for they shall see God."
MATT., chap. v.

CHORUS.

Amen! amen! all richly doth He dower
  Winged Thought, that worm of earth, or bird of sky;
Groveling in slime, or flown, with eagle's power,
  Exultant to the Sun, there to strike bars, and die,
  To rise uncaged—or caged for ever lie.

YOUTH (*addressing the* VIRTUES).

Daughters of God, your heavenly beauty thrills
My soul to ecstasy. Attended thus,
My boat shall dare the billows, like that bird
Of storms, the petrel. Pray ye leave me not;
For when at length the Strait of Death I reach,
Through which Life's sea, all darkly shadowed, runs
On to the Ocean of Eternity,
Despair may rise, from out her loathsome haunt,
And drag me down, as she hath others done.
True is it, that, when Gesmas,* wrecking, called,
Mercy the outcry heard, and sent ye all—
Late calls are risks. Be with me *all* the way.

CHARITY.

Leave thee! ah, never! gentle child of earth,
Unless thou weariest of our company.
But O, beware! Ere long the Vices will
Rise from thy shallop's phosphorescent wake
To haunt persistently, with subtle wile.

---

* The thief converted at the Crucifixion.

O Soul! beloved of Christ, when this shall be,
Heed not their singing. Seal the treacherous ear;
And let the baffled sirens find thee bound,
By thine own hands, with the imperial bands
Of penance, purple-hued. They'll take to wing,
For lakes of fire, with wild despairing cry.

FAITH (*summons* ZEAL).

Zeal! Zeal! Zeal!
O haste! Attend! Attend!
Swoop downward, with strong pinions that outspeed
The lightnings. Lo! The Soul! The Soul in need,
And thou afar, her friend.

Archangel, beautiful!
Christ's banner-bearer, bright!
Thy voice, when warning, like a trumpet note,
When pleading, as Æolian chords that float
To wanderers lost in night.

Zeal presents herself to the Soul, bearing a lyre.

ZEAL (*singing*).

Youth, beware! beware!
And arm with holy prayer.
Temptation comes, in glittering coils, alluring.
Hear not her siren strains,
Wear not her polished chains,
They lead to woe for evermore enduring.

Thou bearest on thy way,
Mantled in fragile clay,
A soul, whose mystic beauty hath enchanted
The GOD, whose Fiat brought
That beauty forth from naught.
O keep it still all lovely and untainted.

Enter Pride, with an air of magnificence.

PRIDE.

Linger, O white-robed Soul! and let me bring
My golden galley to thy fleet barque's side;
The favoring gale fills, with its odorous breath,
My flowing sail. Wilt thou accompany me?
And, as we journey, I will strive to guess
Who thou may'st be, and whither lies thy goal.
A princess, haply—tho' thy robe be plain,
'Tis worn with dignity; and on thy brow
Beameth a jewel, that doth daze mine eyes.

YOUTH.

A "princess"! Yea, by right of that same gem,
Which is not only gem, but also seed
Of future glory. I am homeward bound.

PRIDE.

And where thy home?

YOUTH.

In Heaven's Land of Love.

PRIDE.

I fear me much it is a Land of Myth!
Knowest thou one who hath its beauties seen?
Safer to grasp the Heaven at hand. We *die*.
Thou shalt not sin if thou shalt suffer me
To gild thy barque, to give it silken sail,
Mast of lign-aloes, worth its weight in gold;
If thou, reposeful, on soft cushions thrown,
And followed by obsequious retinue,
Journey as I, and as becomes a queen,
To sunlit seas, that wash the water-stairs
Fronting the ports of Great Jerusalem.

YOUTH.

'Tis a fair picture! but, 'tis often said,
That robes of state hide many a stricken heart.

ZEAL (*advancing sternly*).

Avaunt, thou sophist! Truth Divine hath said,
The camel easier through the needle's eye
May pass than thy vain votaries into Heaven.
Who leaps from eider pillows, to assume
That cross which all must bear to victory?
But late I stood on the volcanic verge
Of the Abyss of Horrors; o'er it hung
A shroud of smoke, black as Egyptian night.
From out that yawning cavern fiercely came
The shriek of blasphemy and mad despair;

And to its mouth, an inky, turbid tide,
Landed, unceasingly, from golden barques,
Unhappy souls that *thou* had'st there decoyed.

 PRIDE (*returning as* ZEAL *retires to background*).
What a fair morn it is! The buoyant Breeze,
All fresh and vigorous—springing from the West,
Hath harnessed to her car the prancing waves,
And tossing their white manes, they sweep along,
Stepping the measure of her monody.
Why choosest thou this unfrequented route?
So unobtrusively thou stealest on,
That fellow-voyagers will surely deem
Thy sail the nautilus.

     YOUTH.
     I am best pleased
To journey thus unnoticed and alone;
But who art thou, that thus dost follow me?

     PRIDE.
Glory, the idol of the great of soul!
Leave this ignoble stream and dare the sea.
Thou art no weed, obedient to the tides—
Scarce sentient polype, bound to coral reef.
Despite the curves of youth and beauty there,
Thought leaves upon thy face her autograph.
Go! take the pen, refresh the world-worn heart
With flash prismatic, from fair Fancy's spray.

Hark, and I'll render thee a nation's boast.
Oft have I snatched the glow-worm from the glebe,
To set it up, for worship, midst the stars.

YOUTH.

Had it been more a star, and less a worm,
It had ambitioned a still loftier throne—
It had despised its base inspiritor.
Perish the hand that hath no higher end
Than man's laudation—oftentimes but smoke
Of interest, flattery, love, or self-conceit!
If the Eternal Wisdom shall decree
Some just compulsion, to make known thy thoughts,
Let them, at least, be odoriferous grains
Of incense, thrown into the thurible,
Swung by the great archangel, standing nigh
The altar of God's glory. He will fill
The golden cup with fire, to cast on earth.

PRIDE.

Take then the lyre, with those whose master-touch
Can send, from quivering string to quivering heart,
Ecstatic thrills of prayer, of pleasure, pain.
Hence! Charm the world with witchery of song.
This morn I saw thy boat bear to the East.
Thou at the prow erect, the rising sun
Beaming upon thy breezy tresses, wreathed
With opening pansies, and, with tuneful lyre
Thou sang'st aloud a glad " Magnificat."

Sweetly it floated to my eager ear,
O'er the elastic waters, fully borne :
No mermaid e'er, in arborescent grot
Of dripping coral, to her pearly shell
Awoke such music.   'Twas the soul of song !
Or write thy name upon the scroll of fame
With sculptor's chisel, or with painter's pen
Bid Science light, through labyrinthian halls.
Arouse, O Youth, to fame !   Why live unknown ?

HUMILITY.

Because, as yet, God hath not called this soul
To use its gifts for others—and, if called,
Because, as man hath nothing of his own,
Save only sin—his powers being all of God,
He should, being known, desire but to be known
As one in whom God may be glorified.
Because all eminence is still a snare
To fallen, tempted man ; because, in fine,
When souls shut off the flaring wicks of earth,
Bright sunrise breaks upon them from the Hills
Eternal ; and they see, in its clear light,
Veiled angels, hidden saints, working the Will
Of a Creator and Redeemer veiled.

SLOTH (*advancing*).

O come and rest !   Thy brow is all bedewed
By o'er-exertion, and heart-struggle draws,
Between the brows, sternly expressive lines.

Thy lips are mute; if vocal, they could tell
Of loneliness, of lacking sympathy,
Of purpose growing weak—temptations strong.
O come and rest! if only for a day;
And yield thyself the luxury of tears.

HOPE *and* CHARITY (*singing*).
O daughter of a king!
Rest not upon the oar.
Eye, ear, and thought have never known
The bliss that waits thy coming home
For evermore.

PLEASURE (*advancing to the Soul*).
How beautiful thou art! Those earnest eyes—
So artless, in their brilliant wonderment—
Enthrall my heart. Young Hebe's blooming cheek
Could scarce have worn such rose-tints as thine own!
Why turn away, sweet ocean sylph? I am
Pleasure, the Queen of Beauty, and my love
For thee is as a sister's. Thou know'st not—
I see it in thy calm, unconscious gaze—
The witchery of loveliness like thine.

ZEAL (*excitedly*).
O Soul beloved! Away! Away with me!
Heed not that glittering serpent. Hedge thine ears!
No safety but in flight! Away! Away!
Alas! thou comest with reluctant step,

And half-averted face, as though a blight
Blasted each aspiration born of Heaven.

PLEASURE (*thrusting Zeal aside*).

Amid the golden beauty of thine hair
Thus let me twine the fair and festal rose.
Embark with us! Behold my Nereids
With choral song and dance; o'er summer seas
The south wind wafts us unto Elysian shores.

Pleasure and Youth, crowned with flowers, dance to that side opposite the Virtues. PLEASURE *sings:*

PLEASURE'S SONG.

Lo! Pleasure, the queen of the free,
  With Beauty and Youth for her prey,
The bowers of Idalia see:
  Come away, come away, come away.
Thou art mine, maiden fair,
By the wreath of red roses that bindeth thine hair.

Leave Thought, by the light of the moon,
  To spin in her mystical cell;
Let Prayer, in her cloisteral gloom,
  The beads of her rosary tell;
Leave Duty and Care,
By the wreath of red roses that bindeth thine hair.

Pleasure dances away with the Soul, followed by Pride, who puts golden chains upon her wrists, and by Sloth, who removes the cross. Chorus of the Virtues:

> O God of Ages! God of Mystery!
> Why, for our life, assume ignoble clay?
> Why die for us on blood-stained Calvary?
> In vain Thy love, Thy sufferings thrown away,
> This Soul is lost!
>
> Coldly she turneth from that Heart Divine,
> Sells Jesus, as the traitor did of old,
> The jewels of His grace are cast to swine.
> Depart, ye angels! Heaven's portals fold!
> The Soul is lost!

Zeal rushes into the midst of the Vices.

I can not calmly see this soul, o'er whom
The Blood and Tears of Jesus have been shed
As water, to eternal ruin borne!
Where'er it goes I follow, and will still
Reproach, and plead, and call on Heaven for aid,
Until it heed that inward monitor,
Who, ever and again, from sleep aroused,
Imperatively speaketh awful truth.

YOUTH.

I can not break this chain. Its coilings mock
My languid efforts. When again I seek

The olden route, voices within, without,
Crave me, in soft, alluring tones, to stay;
And the wild billows, that so oft I've dared
With heart undaunted, strike me with dismay.
Is there no easier way? Must light and shade,
Tempest and calm, for ever alternate
Around the voyager of love and faith?

ZEAL.

Look on the Cross. Plead ye, O precious Wounds!
Your bleeding mouths can utter wondrous words.
O riven Side! tell how the throes of love
Rent thee asunder, more than soldier's lance!
Shame that rose-wreath, O roseate Thorns deep dyed.
Dimmed Eyes, parched Tongue, plead sadly each thy
    cause.

YOUTH.

Too late! The Dove of Mercy leaves the ark;
And here is naught to stay her foot upon.

CHARITY.

Nay, she bears back again the olive-branch—
Thy tears are falling.

FAITH.

               Lo! Thy *Father* waits
With ring and robe, and Mary sweetly pleads.
Hope, take thy lyre! Let all good angels sing:

ANGELS.

Alleluia! Alleluia! Alleluia!
Prostrate before the Throne.
Alleluia! Alleluia! Alleluia!
Mercy receives its own!
As storm-stirred billows of ocean sweep
The circling sands of the striving deep,
So rise ye hosts of the Blest and fling
Your crowns at the Feet of Emanuel—King.
       Alleluia!

Alleluia! Alleluia! Alleluia!
Unto the Trinity—
Alleluia! Alleluia! Alleluia!
Honor and glory be!
In the Holes of the Rock the dove finds rest,
Secure from the vulture's eager quest.
To Him the honor whose Hand hath burst
The meshes that held her pinion fast.
       Alleluia?

THE CROWN OF GLORY.

CHARACTERS REPRESENTED.

ROSALBA, *a Young Artist.*
ERNA, *her Friend.*
OMISSION. ⎫
WEALTH. ⎪
BEAUTY. ⎬ DEPARTED SOULS.
ERUDITION. ⎪
SANCTITY. ⎭
GENIUS.
SPIRIT OF GLORY. ⎫
⎬ APPARITIONS OF THE VISION.
SPIRIT OF MERCY. ⎭
ANGELS IN ATTENDANCE ON SPIRIT OF GLORY.

THE CROWN OF GLORY.

SCENE I.—*Atelier of* ROSALBA. *The artiste sitting thoughtfully before an arch of roses, palette and brush in hand. Enter* ERNA.

    ERNA (*looking at the arch*).
Oh, beautiful! A tasteful floral arch
Of clustering flowers, leaves, and tangling vines—
A model, my Rosalba! And for what?

    ROSALBA.
I shall embower my Flora 'neath that arch.
Ah! I forget. Thou art but late arrived;
And scarce hath heard that Moritz Retzsch* awards
A silver palette to the finest piece
In water-colors. Only residents
Of Dresden can compete. I need not add
How eagerly the prize is coveted,
Nor how enthusiastically strive
The artistes of our famed academy.

---

 * A painter of Dresden, born 1779.

O Heaven, Erna! What a triumph hers
Who shall outpaint the rivals of her school!
And, for that school, from all competitors
Of this great city, bear the palm away.

ERNA.

Ophelia Ullathorne, that English blonde,
Told me of this last eve; and to me showed
The subjects chosen by our artistes. Who
Painted that "Alps at Sunset"? 'Tis well done.

ROSALBA.

The little Marie, Comtesse Vaudémont—
A very dunce; but she can *dance* and *paint.*
Oh! I would give all things beside my soul
To be the victor. Yet, how faint my hope!
Amidst a hundred chances I have one.
Throw back the lattice, Erna! Let the air
Quicken my pulses. I am all unnerved;
And can not hold my pencil. Hast thou seen
Amelia's landscape? Landscapes are her *forte*—
But then she fails in tone. I fear *her* not.
There's Ida's "Ariadne"—mannered—coarse
Of execution— Yea, that Vaudémont
Paints well; and passing well she knows the same.
I can not bear conceit in any one.

ERNA.

I have not seen thy "Flora."

ROSALBA.

                          Nor shall see
Until completed (*clasping her hands and looking toward
   the arch of flowers*). Richly gifted one!
Sweet Carriera,* let thy mantle fall!
Give to thy namesake thy true taste and touch!
In music, letters, I am wont to leave
My compeers far behind. I would once more
Vanquish, though but to chafe my rivals all.
Pray that I do so. I have ceased to pray.
A thousand wild distractions mar my peace.

ERNA.

Thy cheek, but now wan as that withered rose,
Is deeply flushed. Thy dark eyes are aflame.
How sad to see the stormy ebb and flow
Of passion in a soul enslaved to pride!
I, too, in some things can excel, 'tis said.
But, if I watch to keep without my heart
All worthier idols, how much more to keep
Self from the pedestal, from which 'twould flaunt
In its own right, God's gifts gratuitous.
Rosalba, mark thou! This poor heart is small—
A hand could compass it; yet grace shall make
It all too vast for such a deity.
Pride—bane of talent! He who doth excel
Would all excel, and doth so, in his sin.

---

* Rosalba Carriera, a celebrated Italian artiste of the seventeenth century.

But blessed he who, conscious of his gifts,
Knows them as gifts, and consecrates them all
Unto the glorious Giver.   Blessèd he
Who holds the mirror of his mind to Light :
And its clear, shining surface shall reflect
Rays for the guidance of less favored souls.
Like thirst for wine, a thirst for glory is—
Who drinks to quench, a deeper thirst is his.

[*Exit Erna.*

ROSALBA (*painting. Looking at the arch of roses, she murmurs to herself*) :

What for the palette?   That dark Tuscan rose
Will take rich carmine ; and the tendrils, stalks
Of those convolvuli, an emerald green,
With sepia and sienna.   Music !   Where ?

Enter celestial visitant, veiled.   Rosalba falls upon her knees in fear.

APPARITION.

Daughter of earth, look up !   Nay, do not fear ;
Immeasurable love hath sent me here.
Repose thee, while an Artist, dread, divine,
He Who, with sun-rays, gave this earth of thine
The beauteous dyes that blend on sod and sea,
Takes, once again, the brush—for love of thee !

ROSALBA.

What shall I call thee, O Celestial Friend ?

APPARITION.

Enduring Love. Hush! Music! Child, attend!

(*Music. A train of heavenly spirits enter as a retinue to the Spirit of Glory, who, as they take the right and left of the platform, mounts an elevation beneath the arch of roses.*)

Chant of the Spirits. (*Recitative.*)

O Eye of man! Thou wanderest wide,
The glowing earth, the glittering tide.
Day's regal glory, Night's soft grace,
A gem, a flower, a human face,
Can yield thee draughts of beauty deep.
But ah! the golden gates *we* keep
Hide beauties mind may never ween—
Hide beauties eye hath never seen.
O Ear of man! Glad earth, to thee,
Chants pæans of sweet harmony
With wind and string, and song of bird,
With all the strains in nature heard,
With triumph's, joy's, or sorrow's tone.
But ah! the Gates that guard our throne
Re-echo rapturous strains that ear
Of earth could never live and hear.

APPARITION (*pointing to spirits*).

Spirits of Glory, who in radiant state
Around high Heaven's portal coruscate,

Bright cherubs they, who vivid swords unsheath.
He, high exalted, with the gleaming wreath,
Is the great spirit who attends the Throne
With fair immortelles, for the victor grown.

A spirit advances to the center of the stage. Sings:

ASTRAY.

A soul astray! A soul astray!
  Beset by foes, itself a foe.
But 'thwart the gloom a golden ray
  Lights up the dangerous depths below.

A ray of love from Mercy's Throne,
  And on its glory float we here.
Lay thou to heart what thou art shown!
  Lay thou to heart what thou shalt hear!

ROSALBA.

I sleep, of course! And yet 'tis wakeful sleep!
These, then, are of that world invisible,
Before whose majesty we ever move.
Ah! they must view aghast our levity!
Celestial doves, how beautiful ye are!

SPIRIT OF GLORY (*with a passionate gesture*).

O hear! O hear me! Blind and deaf from birth,
Why grovel ye for things that pass with earth?
I stand at Heaven's port—in vain I stand—
Who asks the priceless crown within my hand?

I call, but who my anxious cry can hear—
Earth's echoes dissonant, within the ear?
With woe I watch each generation rise.
Springing from dust, it struggles, fails and dies.
While all expectant, for its hosts, I wait
Its victors jubilant before the gate
Claiming the deathless palm, the spotless stole,
The *Vision Beautiful*, its rest, its goal.
Claiming its Father's long-deferred caress—
Repose, and yet satiety's excess
In that caress, grown God-like, as in light
Of the refulgent sun, a crystal bright.
Gifts scorned, refused—oh, insult, shame, and woe,
Man, stubborn, forces his dark way below.
Who claims the Crown of Glory? Yet once more
I call. Attend ye! Time shall be no more.

APPARITION.

Oh, chilly cold Death's river yonder hies!
Its waves are tears. Its winds regretful sighs,
Through shadowy mists, that pall its waters o'er,
A soul draws nigh, who now may toil no more.
                                [*Enter Omission.*
What is thy name?

OMISSION.

                Omission.

APPARITION.

                        Pass, my friend!
Plead for a crown whose glory hath no end.

SPIRIT OF GLORY.

Omission here! Why! What canst *thou* advance
To prove my gift a due inheritance?
We ask strong blows, for strong our gates are bound;
If thou hast knocked, we have not heard the sound.

OMISSION.

Omission! Yea! Thou rightly hast my name.
Some call me Indolence, 'tis much the same.
I am observant; and have lately seen
That other pilgrims wear a troubled mien—
An air of hesitation, shame or fear,
That scarce would indicate a conscience clear.
Now, *I* have crossed life's vale, and there are none
Can point a finger to an evil done.
I lack, 'tis true, ascetic tastes, ne'er feel
Obliged to set the world ablaze with zeal—
Love mine own ease—float with the tide along.
Do little good; but, then, I do no wrong.
If now and then I fall a precept short,
At least, I am well-clothed, well-bred, well-taught.
And being respectable, would pass your doors;
I do assure ye, devotees are bores.

SPIRIT OF GLORY.

Stand to the left, thou soul without a fear,
And sentence on thy hidden talent hear.

Quartette by the spirits at the gate, as Omission retires to the left.

    Judge between me and my vineyard fair.
        Say, is there aught that I could do more?
    Planted I not of the choicest here?
        Bitterest fruit hath that planting bore!
                          [Enter Wealth.

WEALTH.

I come from halls whose ancient turrets throne
High over towns and hamlets, all their own;
O'er orchards, corn-fields, vineyards hanging low;
O'er woodland vistas haunted by the doe.
My merchant-ships are out upon the sea,
And bear from many a mart and mine to me:

From vaulted halls, whose oriel glories burn
Relics ancestral, portrait, bust, and urn;
And where, 'neath banners o'er escutcheons flung,
The heroes of our house by bards are sung.
Still at my dais, in their liveried state
Obsequious vassals for my beckon wait.

SPIRIT OF GLORY.

What are thy gifts unto the sanctuary?

WEALTH.

The Source of all Gifts looketh not to me.

SPIRIT OF GLORY.

Went forth thy gifts God's poor ones to relieve?

WEALTH.

They, from my heirs, do doubtless *now* receive.

SPIRIT OF GLORY.

The rich, as almoners of Heaven, are sent,
And, false to trust, must look for punishment.
(*Points to the left.*) Go yonder, Wealth, and wait a just decree.
Advance, O Beauty, and prefer thy plea.

ANGELS AT THE GATE (*singing*).

Softly, O wandering Wind!
  The Saviour sleeps.
Around His couch, unkind,
  The chill wind creeps.
Oh, sadly moan,
That sin should thus dethrone
  The God of Love!

Sweet birds, ye have your nests—
  The fox a hole.
But, ah my heart! what rests
  On yon low bole?
A beauteous Head,
O'er which the night-dews shed
  Most bitter tears.

BEAUTY.

Spirit of Glory, I am Beauty—she,
Exalted, as of heaven's nativity,
Rather than earth's.   All hearts confess my sway—
Age, youth, and infancy.   E'en sages gray,
While they would my deceptive spells set forth,
To prove that heart and head alone have worth,
Are tempted, when the casket seems so fair,
To think the pearls of wit and virtue there.
I surely to thy coronal have claim,
For earth on me hath lavished every name
Celestial—"goddess," "angel," "sylph," and "fay"—
I *shall adorn* thy cities' glorious day.
Behold !   What can my grace of form excel ?

SPIRIT OF GLORY (*coolly*).

Java's gay moth—Lattakoo's wild gazelle.

BEAUTY.

Than my fair forehead, what more whitely glows ?

SPIRIT OF GLORY.

The summer lilies and the winter snows.

BEAUTY.

The hair that frames it like a halo's wreath—

SPIRIT OF GLORY.

The silk-worm spins more fine her golden sheath.

BEAUTY.

Have not mine eyes, the poet's song, a charm?

SPIRIT OF GLORY.

More bright the stones that burn upon thy arm.
Stand to the *left*, O Beauty. Frail thy trust—
Food for the tomb, foul rottenness and dust.

Beauty withdraws to the left of the stage. Spirits of Glory sing.

FIRST VOICE.

There is no beauty in Him—see!

SECOND VOICE.

O Grief! The bloody work is mine.

FIRST VOICE.

There is no beauty in Him—He

SECOND VOICE.

Whose human beauty was Divine.

FIRST VOICE.

Why is He thus despised, forlorn?

SECOND VOICE.

Sin struck Him, struck Him, till He died.
Oh, Beauty's source, of beauty shorn!
Pride goes elate, yet deicide.

APPARITION (*pointing*).

Oh, chilly cold, Death's river yonder hies.
Its waves are tears, its winds regretful sighs.
Through shadowy mists, that pall its waters o'er,
A soul draws near, who now may toil no more.
                                        [*Enter Erudition.*

ERUDITION (*to the Spirit of Glory*).

Glory, behold the Pilgrim Erudite.
Mine, mine alone, that crown's ethereal light :
A son of Science, from her temple come,
Much for the mighty goddess have I done,
Haunting her hushed and winding halls, to pore
O'er moldy shrouds of long-forgotten lore.
I through the Future's veils have peered, in vain
Have watched the sun sink, rise, and once more wane,
In cogitating principle, and cause,
Truth, beauty, being, and the wondrous laws
That govern motion, in the mighty race
Of orbs through vast, immeasurable space.
Nature inanimate or animate
Hath not a problem, be it e'er so great,
Unsolvable to me.

SPIRIT OF GLORY (*calmly*).

                Then thou canst tell
Why the pure petals of yon lily-bell
Grew white, whereas its pistil is as gold ?

ERUDITION.

My memory fails me! For a moment hold,
And I will give for this effect the cause—
A simple question, yet, perforce, I pause.

ANGELS AT THE GATE.

O Folly! in the sight
Of Uncreated Light,
   Worlds, clusters, nebulæ,
Are as yon glittering mote
In the sunbeam afloat—
   And thou, what art thou? Say!

Presuming Spirit, hence!
Ah! would that Penitence—
   A teacher kind but stern—
Had shown, ere death, to thee,
Bethlehem's mystery!
   Yet hast thou much to learn.

SPIRIT OF GLORY (*addressing in turn Omission, Wealth, Beauty, and Erudition*).

O Judge of justice! Shall this crown, which cost
The God-man tears and toils, which did exhaust
His burning heart's last life-drop, midst a sea
Of shame, pain, outraged love, Omission's be?
A worm so earthy, that it scarce could learn
To ask for it in prayer, much less to earn.
Angel of Christ's most awful agony,
"Weighed and found wanting" would thy sentence be.

(*To Wealth.*)

Wealth, hear a verity—one apt to shock :
Let Error rave and rage, Truth stands a rock.
God gave thee wealth, which thou didst deem thine own.
How much of it *was* thine ? As much, alone,
As served thy need, and He decreed the rest
The poor man's plunder and the orphan's quest.
It should have gone God's interests to advance,
Battled with sin and banished ignorance ;
But 'twas thy god. Banks bore, by thy control,
While for a crust a brother begged or stole ;
Clasped thy fair sheen of silk and velvet fine
With gems, prismatic-hued, from wave and mine,
While foul and bony went he, shivering past,
His tattered rags contending with the blast.
God willed not this, but destined thee to be
Steward to the starving—and doth now from thee
Require their tears, their sadly darkened lives.
Sin-stained with Dives, go hence and weep with Dives !

(*To Beauty.*)

Depart, O Beauty ! Might we give to thee
The Crown of Glory, it would justly be
The right of beast and bird, of flower and fly.
It wreathes not loveliness that blooms to die.
Thou shouldst, in life, have learned from the device
Of those bright birds, so called of paradise,
That seem of sunsets born, and made to bear
Their glories miniatured to lower air ;

They fly not *with* the breeze, which rudely blows
Their clouds of plumage, purple, golden, rose,
Around them ; but they wait an adverse wind,
Which throws their hindering splendors far behind.

(*To Erudition.*)

Thou, Erudition, arrogant o'er theft
From mighty minds of Past and Present reft ;
Thou of the subtile intellectual thought,
The glowing dream in realms of fancy wrought ;
What didst thou with the gifts of thy grand soul?
Winged they the sun-bright wheels that onward roll
The chariot of God's glory? Was it thine
With reverence to unveil the ways divine?
Nay, thou didst seek but to usurp thy Lord :
How dar'st *thou* claim the crown of His reward?
O Judge of justice ! sanction my decree.
Art thou the bliss eternally to be
Of souls who scorned in time Thy law and Thee?

[*The Spirits of Glory answer on the part of God.*

ANGELS AT THE GATE (*in recitative*).

A voice responds : O Spirits, bend ye low !
From the Dread Throne the vivid lightnings flow.
Angels unsheathe their swords, and Justice answers,
  " No ! "

SPIRIT OF GLORY.

Ye Hierarchies, all jubilant and grand,
That, host on host, in flashing splendors stand

Around your King, with those fair companiments,
Apostles, Martyrs, Virgins, Innocents,
Will ye receive these bats and birds of night
In light, to gaze upon Eternal Light?

ANGELS AT THE GATE.

Hark, sister Spirits! hark ye! From afar,
Portals of pearl and diamond unbar;
From lyres of gold the sweetest numbers flow,
And tongues like wind-swept forests answer, "No!"

SPIRIT OF GLORY.

O Man! O slumbering man! when wilt thou wake?
When wilt thou learn the awful prize at stake?
When wilt thou strive, with violence, to be
Heir of this crown, of this celestial key,
Grace-consummated? Lo! it casteth wide
Flood-gates of bliss, whose vast, o'erwhelming tide
Would sweep the soul to naught, were it not stayed
By that Right Hand, which thrones the soul, arrayed
In joy immutable, far, far above,
Endowed with science—vision, seraph's love—
Its casket changed—the once ignoble clay
Now swift and subtile, as light's living ray—
That Hand which gives it Mary's realm and kiss
Bears it yet higher—oh, ecstatic bliss!
Until 'tis lain, transfixed with love's last dart,
In ravished peace upon the Sacred Heart.

EVENINGS AT SCHOOL.

ANGELS AT THE GATE (*in recitative*).

Man heeds ye not. Let Nature, reasonless,
Lift up its voice, and the Creator bless.
Let her in dirges, sadly, sweetly poured,
Mourn for her master man, her fallen lord.

Dirge for Lost Souls.

Ye mighty billows, stormy ocean o'er,
Sweep ye, in grand funereal march, to shore;
Cast yourselves on it, with despairing fall.
Man's heart is rock! In vain Love's tender call.
    And when the tide of woe
    Subsides to calmer flow,
    To bright-hued shell and stone
Go murmur in thine own complaining tone.

Arise, ye winds! and sing a requiem wild,
In ancient forests, greenly arched and aisled,
Gracefully swaying, as thy wings sweep by
With myriad pulses, thrilling to the cry;
    Or sink, in smothered sobs,
    O'er sin that heaven robs,
    And sigh, with fitful breath,
O'er souls that Death must give to endless death.

Drape slowly, somberly, ye clouds, the skies;
Why should the stars with their bright holy eyes
Look on their fallen sister, midst the spheres?
Shed o'er her, then, a passion of wild tears.

O man! and can it be?
God died for love of thee—
Created of the sod
And thou—oh, weep, sad skies—*man loves not God!*

During the singing of the Dirge, four cherubim, with swords of gold, motion Omission, Wealth, Beauty, and Erudition from the scene.—Enter Sanctity and Innocence.

APPARITION.

Ye angels, on the battlements intone
Your anthems. Lo! fair Sanctity comes home—
God's well-beloved. Go harping forth and meet
That ardent heart, which like a censer sweet
Burned for God only, till its sweet desire
Outflashed to wandering souls, the sacred fire:
That lowly heart, so calm, so meek, so pure,
Content to labor, patient to endure;
That chastened heart, in which self daily died
Before the image of the Crucified.

SPIRIT OF GLORY.

Ere thou dost enter, tell us by what right,
O Sanctity! Because thy robe is white?
Because of charity to God and man?
Because of heavenly life on earth began?

SANCTITY.

Why should I plead my Saviour's gifts to thee?
He died that mine your diadem should be.

In holy hope, I washed in Calvary's flood,
Open, in right of Christ's most precious Blood!

CHORUS.

*While Sanctity is crowned, and passes through the arch of
roses, the Chorus, to livelier time, sings:*

THOU WAST ESPOUSED UNTO THE KING.

Thou wast espoused unto the King,
   The crown is therefore thine of right;
Thou art a conqueress, and doth bring
   With thee the trophies of thy might.
Thou didst with patience weave
   Thy bridal raiment. It is done—
The silver warp from Eve,
   The golden woof from Mary's Son.

    [*Innocence advances, with a dove in her arms.*

SPIRIT OF GLORY.

Ah! little birdling, fluttering from the nest,
Thou seekest early thy Great Father's Breast,
And standest gazing on my circlet bright,
As though there were no question of *thy* right.
With scarlet lips, that part o'er pearls beneath;
With ringlets bound by snowy rose-bud wreath;
With blue eyes raised in sweet, confiding love;
And dimpled arms entwined around thy dove,*

---

* Spirit of Glory, supposed to allude to a child's state and intention, at the moment of death.

Thou comest to the gate, as thine own bird,
Unto its vine-hung nest, by zephyrs stirred.

CHILD.

The Infant Jesus asketh naught of me—
His love requiring only that I be
Bathed in the ruby founts of Calvary.—Lo !
I washed, and now to Mary's Babe would go.
And, as I sank to sleep, I saw my dove,
And brought him hither, as a gift of love,
Around his neck an azure ribbon tied.
The Boy Divine shall have him—none beside.

SPIRITS OF GLORY (*chant*).

" Suffer children to come unto Me, and forbid them not,
For of such is the kingdom of God.
Whoever shall not receive the kingdom of God as a child,
Shall not enter into it."

SPIRIT OF MERCY (*taking Rosalba by the hand, leads her to the Spirit of Glory*).

ROSALBA (*shrinking back in terror*).

Where wouldst thou lead?—To Judgment? Nay, depart!
Life, though it freeze with horror, in my heart
Still beats there faintly.—Dead?—I still have breath.
Unveil, dread shade! I fear thee! Art thou Death?

SPIRIT OF GLORY (*with irony*).

Genius at Judgment! Eaglet of the skies!
The limit of whose flight that line which lies

Where loftiest human thought doth flag her wings,
And thought angelical the lowliest springs?
Whose sparkling pen electric flashes brought
From slumbering nations—Thought's response to thought;
Who, when worn Nature respite would entreat,
Lured with the lyre all hearts unto her feet;
Caught on her canvas all the loveliness
Relation, truth, and likeness, there express—
Great gifts gratuitous of heaven's King.
What, with them, hath she wrought? What doth she bring?
Hath she no cross-signed offering from the strife?

ROSALBA.

O empty hands! O wasted grace and life!
Where canst thou turn, Rosalba, hope to find?
Have pity, Lord, for I was blind, blind, blind!

CHORUS OF SPIRITS.

GO HENCE, O GENIUS.

Go hence, O Genius, for thy sin
    Exhales to heaven the foulest breath.
Was there no voice, thy soul within
        To disenchant?
To tear from eyes, so penetrant,
    The knotted fillet of eternal death?

Go hence, and weep, for God designed
    Thy soul to be a temple grand,

THE CROWN OF GLORY.

    Wherein the stately powers of mind
        In solemn rite
    Should offer from their censers bright,
      And move, all beautiful, at His command.

      ROSALBA (*falling on her knees*).

Have mercy, Heart of Christ—sweet mercy's Source!
Love tears my heart with passionate remorse;
O Lord, I loved Thee, though no service gave;
Ora pro me, sweet Mother, plead to save!

      APPARITION (*removing the veil*).

Thou callest Mercy. She is ever nigh;
Its sacred symbol on my heart doth lie.
I bring the pardon which it doth outpour.
Forget not Mercy. Go, and sin no more.

      SPIRIT OF GLORY (*to Rosalba*).

Ah! Genius, Beauty, Rank—rare trinity,
Would that ye came more often unto me!
Go, soul, and later bring unto their Source
Those gifts, oft misapplied, to man's remorse.
Go back, transfigured, robed with grace and light,
Thy royal purple guarding spotless white.
                  [*Sanctity enters arch.*
Come, Sanctity, a queen, and reign above!
                  [*Innocence enters arch.*
Come, Innocence, as guileless as thy dove!
God yet shall call *thee*, O repenting Love.

56 EVENINGS AT SCHOOL.

CHORUS BY SPIRITS OF GLORY,

During which Rosalba, led by Mercy, retires to the place which she occupied before the occurrence of the vision. She kneels, with her hands clasped over her face.

TAKE THE CROWN.

Take the crown! Take the crown!
But the hand of the Lord

Must encircle thee round,
When its glory is poured;

THE CROWN OF GLORY.

For, as forests aflame to the parched blade of grass,
So torrents of joy o'er thy spirit must pass.
        To the gate's ambient hush
        Float ye up, midst the rush
        Of white, scintillant wings—
Of pure foreheads, star-crowned, aureoled with light;
        Float ye up, midst the gush
        Of a thousand sweet strings.

        Spirit Light! Spirit Love!
          With thy jubilant fire,
        Teach us praise. O thou Dove!
        Be our spirits thy lyre.
In exile the Three could not meetly be praised;
'Twas the Heart of the Host that our anthems upraised.
        To the gate's ambient hush
        Float ye up, midst the rush
        Of white, scintillant wings—
Of pure foreheads, star-crowned, aureoled with light;
        Float ye up, midst the gush
        Of a thousand sweet strings.
            [*Mercy and the Spirits of Glory vanish.*

        Enter ERNA.

Rosalba! Rose! She's lost in some sweet dream.
I never saw her look so beautiful!
What ails thee, maiden? Thy large eyes are wide,
With a far look of reverent wonderment;
Thy pallid lips move mutely. Art thou faint?

ROSALBA.

Oh, hush! The place is holy. I have seen—
O Erna! Erna!—I have seen the gate
Of heaven open. I have heard its songs
And drank its golden airs—aroma-filled—
Have gazed on deathless flowers, that kissed the feet
Of empyrean forms, divinely fair:
I, who have trodden, with defiant foot,
That path which slopes to hell's abyss, and hung
O'er its fierce fires, suspended by a breath!
I, haunted ever by a pleading voice,
Now loud, imperative, now sweet-toned, low,
As to arrest me e'en despite my will,
Have seen in vision a dread monitor—
A King in bloody bonds, with godlike mien,
That cast me prostrate. Ah! those tender Eyes!
They haunt me yet. He raised a Wounded Hand,
Signed to His clotted cross, His thorny crown,
Then drew aside His vesture.—Girl, I saw
A Heart on fire, and deeply riven through!
Oh, 'tis my home, and I am homesick long.
I henceforth am its psalmstress: for my soul
Was formed a lyre, high hung, upon whose chords
Nature might give to God sweet minstrelsy;
Yea, and its vot'ress, vowed unto the search,
Along life's pathway, for all scattered pearls
Of its pure glory—reparatrix, too,
To mourn, whene'er I see sin beating out

God's blessed Image in the souls He loves.
How much I have to do—ay, and undo!
Depart, dear Friend, and leave me to myself—
To think, to pray, and peacefully to weep.—
Christ, loving God, this contrite heart shall be
Henceforth a "crown of glory" wreathed for Thee.

THE ENCHANTED ISLE.

CHARACTERS.

BIANCA.	VITTORIA.
GIOVANNA.	GABRIELLA.
IPPOLITA.	MARIA.
HERMIONE.	LUCIA.
RAPHAELLA.	CORNELIA.
SANTA ROSALIA.	BEATRICE.
LUGIA.	

THE ENCHANTED ISLE.*

BIANCA.

The Enchanted Isle! the Enchanted Isle, at last!
Cornelia, furl the sail, and make it fast;
There lies our wake, the wayward waters o'er.
We port! we port! Come, maidens, leap ashore.
O pretty boat! O buoyant "Golden Shell," †
Rock lightly there, until Palermo's bell,
Soft tolling o'er Tyrrhenia, sweetly calls
Its errant maids to their ancestral halls.

GIOVANNA.

Mysterious isle! How silently it lies!
Bathed in the rose-tints of Sicilian skies.
Those groves of cypress, clambering up the steep;
Those circling waters, murmuring as they creep;
The very winds seem, with uplifted hand,
To warn me, passing, "This is spirit-land!"
There is a weird look in the wild-bird's eye—
Scrolled secrets in the shells that scattered lie;

---

* Monte Pellegrino.
† Conca d'Oro, the plain on which the city of Palermo is built.

And Fancy hears far-distant music break
From the rock-chaliced waters of yon lake.

IPPOLITA.

Relying not upon mine reticence,
Ye would not give to me your confidence,
And if one of your merry crew I make,
It was permitted for Bianca's sake,
My sister ; but ye promised to reveal
The secret of your project, when the keel
Of the "Golden Shell" these waters should divide.
Disclose it now, and by your word abide.
Rest ye awhile, and here resolve to me
Why thus twelve noble maids of Sicily
Steal from their homes, with unavowed design,
And, with patrician hands, so fair and fine,
Pilot their own frail shallop, to intrude
On Pellegrino's upper solitude.

HERMIONE.

See ! Ippolita, yonder misty steep
High jutting o'er the ever-striving deep
Is, at the vertex, somewhat like a stall
Seen in a cloister choir. Old legends call
It "Rock of Destiny"; and it is said
That she who looks from thence, when, lightly sped,
The moon's first beam upon the billow lies,
Shall see her future, like a mirage, rise.
Lo ! we are hither come, with firm resolve
To test assertion, and a mystery solve.

RAPHAELLA.

Doth our audacious intent strike thee mute?
Not *too* much valor to the brave impute.
If, in each heart, there lurks an undefined
Faith in the preternatural, 'tis entwined
With equal growth of skepticism—we
Not wiser, for our quest, expect to be:
We buy at least the right to, later, boast
That we have dared the phantoms of the coast.
But, lo! at last, we've clomb to sight of sea—
I stand upon the Rock of Destiny!

(*Enter Santa Rosalia,* who suddenly confronts them.*)

SANTA ROSALIA.

Rise! and fear not. Rosalia ye behold,
To whom, so oft, your sorrows have been told
In Pellegrino's cave. Why come you here
To question those who may no more appear?
Should Christians seek old pagan oracles?
Your wondering horror, now contrition tells—
Ye knew not what ye did—yet knew ye not
That this, to youth, is a forbidden spot?
O disobedient! Doth not Holy Church
Forbid her child, by occult means, to search

---

* St. Rosalia was a Norman princess, who retiring to the grotto of Monte Pellegrino, a rocky mass in the northwest of the city of Palermo, passed there her life in prayer and good works. She is patroness of Palermo.

The Future's misty realm? Can demons show
That which puissant angels may not know?
With wisest love, God curtains from our ken
The paths that traverse it; for, fallen man
Must suffer to be saved. Death's Conqueror,
With the red Cross, forced back high Heaven's bar:
All who would pass, with Him, that glorious keep,
Must storm it cross-signed, or forever weep.
Who safely woes impending could behold,
E'en tho' revealed the graces that they hold?
Who, undespairingly, could contemplate
The scathing tempests that, corrective, wait
Our guiltiness—the demon-haunted gloom
Which hell sends forth from out her living tomb
To be the test of virtues? Who would gaze
Forth to those years when busy Time shall raze
And shroud our hopes and loves—shall show the rent
Of every broken reed on which we leant?
Can ye not better bear to, one by one,
Count his thick graves, than die before their sum?
"And are there none," ye ask, "who might behold
A future like yon sunset fair outrolled?"
There are: but she who in her future lives,
The present scorning, to her Maker gives
No perfect work. The sculptor's stone, abject,
Which Time alone can chisel and perfect,
Seeing itself to god-like glory grown,
Would fain forget the present's shapeless *stone*.
In punishment of your temerity,

Ye *shall* the secrets of that Future see ;
And, lest the revelation's weight oppress,
I have obtained, for your unguilefulness,
That, with the cross, shall also be revealed
The kernel sweet, its armèd burrs concealed.
Lo ! the moon rises, and her silvery bow
Doth, o'er the deep, a glittering arrow throw.—
Look forth, Vittoria ! What dost thou behold ?

VITTORIA.

Naught but the vesper star, so far, so cold—
Stay ! What is *that?* Mists gather o'er the wave.
They meet—they part—a grand cathedral nave,
Filled with the mightiest of Church and state—
What is the regal rite they celebrate ?
Down through the gorgeous, many-colored lights
The sunlight throws its splendor, and unites
With flash of gems on cope and miter shed ;
With flash of gems on many a graceful head ;
On mail-clad men ; on banners, plumes, and spears.
They crown a king ! And lo ! his queen appears.
How lovely is she ! But how wan ! how cold !
That *face!* It is *myself* that I behold !

SANTA ROSALIA.

It *is* thyself, and thou dost well to mark
That cold thy cheek, and passionless and dark.
The lowly may, unblamed, give sorrow breath ;
The lofty smile—and bleed within, to death !

THE ENCHANTED ISLE.

(Motioning forward Gabriella, and addressing her.)

Thy jeweled vest, and flowing velvet robe,
Thine ostrich-plumèd cap, with diamond lobe,
Are but ill chosen for thine enterprise.
Thou art a tulip, child; but other skies
Shall fashion thee a violet of the grass,
Breathing out odors unto all that pass.
Mount thou the rock—look forth upon the sea,
And what its vapors picture, tell to me.

GABRIELLA.

I see the cottage of an artisan.
A patient woman, poorly clad, and wan,
Toiling amid the poor, her threshold worn
By feet to want, to pain, to sorrow born—
To all a solace, while she yearns for One
To call: "'Tis consummated. Daughter, come!"
I poor in age! O Gabriella, weep!
Better a thousand times that thou shouldst sleep
'Neath the deep waves that wash this fatal rock—
Nay, leave me, friends; your consolations mock.
Heiress of Valenzano's ducal line,
Must toil and penury like this be mine?

SANTA ROSALIA TO MARIA AND RAPHAELLA.

Kneel ye together; for ye are akin
In Christ, if not in Adam.

MARIA.

                    Mists begin
To gather from the east. Behold, they wreath
Into a Gothic archway; from beneath
A virgin issues forth, with modest grace,
In quaint religious garb, her thoughtful face
Smiling upon an orphan at her side.
Through darkened haunts, where Want and Sin abide,
She passes midst the poor, the sick, the sad,
As pass the sunbeams, beautiful and glad.
The cross she kisses of her rosary—
Her daily cross, for God borne generously.
Above her angels, and, amid them, one
Who holds a crown which doth outgleam the sun.
What! I a daughter of sweet Charity?
Avert it, saint! It shall not, must not be:
None must, perforce, such mountain paths aspire—
O mother fond! O brothers, sisters, sire!
My heart-strings hold you with a hundred ties.
Vision, away with thine alluring guise!
Vanish, ye falsehoods of a vaporous breath—
Maria leave her home?—She will—in death!

RAPHAELLA.

I hear the chiming of an abbey-bell,
I see a minster's ivy-mantled cell:
A nun within, in sable robe and veil;
Much prayer and many fasts have worn her pale.

What doth that glance, so pure and pleading, fix?
The fiery Heart upon her crucifix.
That Raphaella?—giddy, vain, and gay,
Whose fairy feet oft danced the night away;
Who loves to see her beauty bright enthrall
The brilliant throng of boulevard and ball?
Perhaps one beholds another's destiny!

SANTA ROSALIA.

Not so! What God hath spoken, yet shall be.

BIANCA.

Ye viewless spirits of this haunted rock,
Bianca's fearless soul ye shall not shock!
No wealth hath she to lose, nor would she wail
If her plain face were shrouded in a veil!
Good Heavens! I almost fell into the sea.
Who is that lady looking up at me?
How rich, how ready is her lavish hand,
To all the poor that throng at her command!
Above her brow, a starry legend gleams—
(The brow is mine, whate'er the legend means)
" Not long need Want entreat, nor Woe adjure
The gentle mother of Palermo's poor!"

LUCIA.

Seest thou that girl?—myself, of course, I stand
Upon a festooned dais, lute in hand,
Warbling to royalty. A thousand rise!
And Lucia's name is lauded to the skies.

Amid her floral offerings, how she bends
With gracious smile! But see! A chasm rends
Beneath her feet, and sulphurous clouds upcurl.
She totters—falls! Oh, some one save the girl!
Why stop they not their plaudits? Can't they see
They *encore* her to endless misery?
She vanishes! I heard her call a name:
"Maria, pray!" and lo! the hungry flame
Fair Virgin feet out-trampled. Let me go
And rest me yonder. Ah! I tremble so.
You whisper, "'Twas myself!" Yes! yes! I know.

CORNELIA.

Lead Lucia hence! Come, maidens, quick, to me.
Look where I point! Canst see what I now see?
'Twas there! 'Tis gone! Oh, no! 'Tis present now—
A Muse with scroll, green bays upon her brow.
She cons the learned page with weary eyes,
Till Dawn bears hence the tapers of the skies;
In schools to wisdom sacred she is heard;
Sage doctors hang intent on every word.
Her laurel, long ambitioned, Time concedes—
She grasps: 'tis thornless, yet she shrinks—she bleeds
Too *late to win*, a greater prize appears:
The first she heeds not, blinded by her tears.

BEATRICE.

Come, Lugia love, the Rock shall show to thee
An active life of rich utility.

Thou busy Lugia, of a hundred plans,
Health, wealth, rank, beauty—all are in thine hands.

LUGIA.

Lo! the moon shrouds. The waves are darkly decked,
As though a floating pall above the wrecked.
Why dirge they thus, forever moving on?
They rise in shadowy mists. I gaze upon
A long funereal train, with torch and bier.
Speak low! speak low! The dead is passing near.
O sweet, pale face!—a girl! So young to die!
Stand back! give air! I faint! 'Twas I, 'twas I!

SANTA ROSALIA.

Go hence, 'tis morn—life's morn for all, save one ;
Go hence, with prayer—*this prayer*, "Thy will be done!"
Ye are not singular amid your kind :
All may gaze here, and still some marvel find.
Go to life's duties with a purpose high :
For God and heaven to live, to love, to die.
And should thy path be ever smooth and fair,
Tremble. Angelic footsteps are not there.
But if, at times, with rock and bramble sown,
Press on. The Heart of Christ is near thine own.
Worship the world not. 'Tis destined for the tomb—
Wealth, beauty, genius, aid not at the doom.
And sit not idle. Ere the world was made,
Apportioned was thy task—thy field outlaid ;
None but thyself can in its furrows plod.

Pass from it up with golden sheaves for God.
Life's an uneasy dream ; we wake, when o'er,
To find the real upon the farther shore.
Come hence, my children ! Hark the compline-bell !
I'll take the helm of your frail " Golden Shell,"
And, while we sail, sing sweetly all with me,
"Wisdom and Love Divine, we trust in Thee ! "

THE MUSIC OF A MORNING DREAM.

MELODRAMA FOR CHILDREN.

CHARACTERS.

Ice-King.
Ether, the Empress.
The Spirits of the Flowers.
The Spirits of the Sunbeam.
The Spirits of the North Wind.
Spirit of Air.
Spirit of Dew.
A Dryad, the Spirit of the Willow-Tree.

THE MUSIC OF A MORNING DREAM.

PROLOGUE.

The meaning of our piece, in prose, is this:
Air, saturated, brings its vapor nigh
Unto the rose, and her cool leaves condense
That vapor into dew; then come the winds
And bear the glistening drop to the chill North.
Frost chains it there, till Ether, swift, transmits
The Sunbeam, with the seven latent hues
Of the solar spectrum. By heat's potency,
Dew crystallized is vapor once again.
Here Poetry comes in, with Pythian pipe,
And sings *her* version—her sweet morning dream:
Air woos a vapor from the ocean wastes,
And bears her to the bosom of the Rose.
The Queen Flower's kiss transforms the misty maid,
And she becomes the Spirit of the Dew.
Enter the boisterous winds, the Storm-King's band;
They bear her to the dungeons of the North.

The Sunbeam pleads, the stern Ice-King relents ;
And to the drooping flowers gives the Dew.

SCENE I.—*Woodland bower. Throne of the Rose in the center. The Queen Flower enters, followed by her attending Spirits.*

SPIRIT OF THE LILY.

Here, in this garden of Bahrein fair,
We've built thee a bower, of roses that bear,
  In pathways of paradise, lost.
Beautiful Rose Spirit, mount to a throne,
Whose festoons and garlands have never been strewn
  By Spirit of Wind or of Frost.

SPIRIT OF CAMELLIA.

Beautiful Rose Spirit, see ! we have here
Blossoms that grew on the mounts of Cashmere,
  From seeds that were gathered, ere sin
Blighted all beauty with poisonous breath,
Brought to all nature decadence and death:
  We wreathe thy fair forehead within.

SPIRIT OF THE ANEMONE.

Bow down your heads, Spirits all, to the Rose ;
Dance, waving wands, while the trumpet-flower blows.
  All the vines hanging on high,
With leaves for your tambours, with tendrils for wires,
Sing sweet to the Rose, on Æolian lyres,
  A chorus as 'round her we fly.

Song of the Flower Spirits.

Wear the crown, royal Rose!
Lovely queen!
Reign for aye, over those
Who, unseen,

Haunt the forest-tree and flower—
Spirits born of Helios' power.
    Crown the Rose!

Would ye, Flower Spirits, see
 Mortal bold?
Not in taste or tint are we.
 They but hold
Our frail being, our sweet breath—
We, the flowers' life and death.
    Crown the Rose!

SPIRIT OF CONVOLVULUS.

Music! sweet music! I hear it, afar.
Hither rides Air, on her thistle-down car.
    [*Enter Zephyr.*

ROSE QUEEN.

Welcome, sweet Zephyr, thou comest in glee,
From haunts on the hills where the heather-bells be.
Spirits of flowers, with rapturous sigh,
Rustle their leaves, as your lute warbles by.
Why seek this isle of Iranian seas?
Come you to crown me, sweet Sylph of the Breeze?

SPIRIT OF AIR.

Lady, I knew that the elves of the flowers
Flew to your fêting in Bahrein's bowers:
Seeking a gift that might gladden thine eyes,
I wandered earth's waters, her woodlands and skies.

Nature had naught that the Rose could commend—
Almost despairing, I thought of a *friend.*
Queen of the Flowers, thou knowest I reign
Over the sylphs of the mountain and main ;
Blowing our silvery trumpets, we ride
Landward and seaward. To-day, on the tide,
Saw we the Sprites of the Sunbeam at play,
Coaxing the shy little Vapors away.
Snatching this nymph from a child of the Sun,
Hither I brought her, O beautiful one !
Bashfully hides she her face from your view :
Ocean-elves call her the " Vapor of Dew."

ROSE.

Oh, she is sweet, but she never will stay !
E'en as I speak, she is floating away.

AIR.

Clasp her ! embrace her ! O royal red Rose !
Let her veiled cheek on thy bosom repose.
Kisses transform her. She falls on thy breast,
Trembling and laughing—Love's lure is the best.
Ever thine handmaid, baptize her anew.

ROSE.

Vapor no more. She is maid Morning Dew.

DEW (*singing to Air, who, with her sylphs, is departing*).
Zephyr, that bore me o'er land and o'er sea,
Fare-thee-well ! Fare-thee-well ! Fare-thee-well !

AIR AND HER SYLPHS.

Many a mask shall the Rose give to thee.
Morning Dew, fare-thee-well! fare-thee-well!

SCENE II.—*A forest. Enter, on one side, Spirit of the Dew, sprinkling the earth from a vase; on the other a Dryad.*

DRYAD.

Many a woodland I've followed thee through,
Daughter of calm Night, beneficent Dew.
Tracking you still, by the jewels you cast
Out of your urn as you rapidly passed.
Fleet-footed ever, more fleet must you be:
Danger is coming, for you and for me!

DEW.

Green-mantled maiden, who art thou, I pray?
And what is the danger that chides my delay?

DRYAD.

Dryad am I, and this willow-tree's life.
All these tall oaks have their wood-spirits blithe:
See how they tremble, wild tossing their leaves;
See how they whisper, as mourner that grieves.
Fleet-footed ever, more fleet must thou be:
Danger is coming, for you and for me!

DEW.

Danger—from whence?

DRYAD.

      Look, thou, far out at sea!
The North King approaches, with wild revelry.
The coursers of ocean his goblins bestride;
Careering and plunging, they lash as they ride.
Alas for the beautiful aisles of the wood!
The ash and the oak, that have centuries stood.

Enter North King and Storm Spirits, singing.

Away! away! on the storm-wind's breath,
   We are rushing forth!
   We are hurrying forth!
To the Ice-King's realm, where all is death—
To the North! to the North! to the frozen North!

They catch up the Spirit of Dew and bear her away. Enter
ROSE.

Maid of the Willow, thou weepest, and why?

DRYAD.

Heardst thou the gnomes of the North Wind go by?

ROSE.

Yea. Have they wasted your palace of green?

DRYAD.

Havoc and ruin are everywhere seen.
Not for myself do I sigh, but for *you*.
Know, they have captured your handmaid, the Dew.
Passing this morn, on my way to the height,

I saw her bedewing the buttercup bright :
Suddenly passed the wild sprites of the North—
Blinded by tear-drops, they carried her off.

ROSE (*to her attending Spirits*).

Flower Spirits fair, of my radiant realm,
Low bow your heads, and let sorrow o'erwhelm.
Mourn, lovely flowers—the Spirit Queen mourns ;
Take my red diadem—deck me with thorns.
Lost is my maiden, the tried and the true ;
Friend of my bosom—dear Diamond Dew.

DRYAD.

See ! A dark spot on the disk of the sun
Opes, as a gate ; and its vivid rays run
Down to the earth, like a road without end :
On it a thousand swift spirits descend.
Ether approacheth, the Empress of Light ;
Ruler of elfins who, rapid and bright,
Golden lamps bring from the great orb of day ;
Silver lamps bring from the moon's pensive ray ;
Sovereign beside of those phantom-like hosts,
Delving in rocks, of the wild ocean-coasts,
With phosphoric torches ; and Queen of the Sprites
Bearing the flashing electrical lights.

[*Enter Ether and Sun Spirits.*

ROSE.

Mistress supreme, of the day's golden hours,
Why hast thou sought the sad Queen of the Flowers ?

ETHER.

Even to kiss her, as always each morn;
Seeking yet further her grace to adorn—
Yea, and to aid her, if drooping in pain.
Favorite, ask of your fond suzerain.

ROSE.

Give me again the sweet Maid of the Dew,
Torn from my heart by the Wind-Monarch's crew.
She in the cells of the Ice-King is cast,
Fetters of crystal, there, binding her fast.

ETHER.

Look at this prism—this gem I have here.
Triple its facets, as diamond clear.
If to the sun I thus hold it aside,
Out of its angle a door opens wide.
Spirits pass out, born of Ether and Sun,
Garbed in the gayest of mantles each one—
Hither they come, and great artistes are all.
Ye seven wise daughters, attend to my call!
These the fair maidens, O royal Rose Queen,
Who in your gardens are oft to be seen,
Sitting on sun-birds, and painting the flowers;
Riding on rain-drops, to paint after showers
Noe's bow of Hope. When the day calmly dies,
Drop they her couch in the far western skies.
Sometimes they hie to the mermaiden's cells,
Tinting her coral and touching her shells;

Sometimes the gem, in deep cavern immured;
Sometimes the wing of the paradise-bird.
Now in the sunbeam they haste to unchain
The captive Dew-fay, and restore her again.

SCENE III.—*Hall of the Ice-King, who, throned, receives the Spirits of the Sunbeam.*

ICE-KING.

Spirits of Sunlight, ye come without call,
Forcing your way to the Ice-Monarch's hall."

THE RED RAY (*one of the Spirits*).

Ice-King! we sprites of the solar spectrum,
By Ether's command, to your presence have come.
Bound, in your palace of ice and of snows,
Thou hast the Dew-drop, beloved by the Rose.
Prythee, release her! The Flowers despair:
She decked them in all the bright jewels they wear;
Morning and evening they wither and pine—
We pray thee, great monarch, the maiden resign.

ICE-KING.

That will I not! She now dwelleth among
The Elves of the Snow, by the poets oft sung.
Often with them from the storm-cloud she vaults,
Chasing and whirling, in bacchanal waltz;
Often, a beautiful statue, she sleeps
In crystalline caves, that the Frost Spirit keeps.

Yesterday, roving aloft, was she found
By spirits electric. They caught her, and bound
With hundreds of others that happened to pass,
And hurled them to earth, locked in globules of glass.
There, in the snow-fields, the Dew Maiden lies;
And she, of you seven, with sharp enough eyes,
Dew-drop to choose, and to take by the hand,
From thousands as like as are atoms of sand,
May claim her, and bear her again to the Rose,
With all of such heart as an Ice-Monarch knows.

RED RAY (*pointing to the Dew*).

There lies the captive, as lifeless as stone!
Few things, O monarch, are secrets unknown
To Sunbeam and Air. The strong spells of her bond
We quickly o'ercome by the touch of our wand.
Once do I touch her, the spell is undone;
Twice do I touch her, she leaps to the Sun—
Spreading her winglets, fast gaining their growth,
Vapor again shall she voyage the South.

ICE-KING.

Not so fast! potent Spirits of Sunbeam, of heat,
North Winds shall cut off the maiden's retreat.

SPIRITS OF THE SUNBEAM.

North Winds are strong; but the Sun stronger still;
Its arrows can alter their currents at will—
Expanding, contracting, the air as they wend.
Oh, Dew-drop is ours, and the Dream is at end.

88   EVENINGS AT SCHOOL.

SONG.

ZEPHYR.

Unchain the Dew—the Rain,
Winds of the North!

WINDS.

With threatening growl, and with sudden roar,
We bid you hence from our ice-bound shore;
For the Dew and Rain shall return no more—
Shall ne'er go forth.

ZEPHYR.

Hark to the chorus sweet
Of the dying flowers!

FLOWERS.

We thirst and we droop under every sky!
Give rain and dew, or the flowers die—
To teach, no more, the wanderer by
    Of heaven's bowers.

ICE-KING.

Bear the Morning Dew to the Rose,
    Zephyr—sweet lute!

WIND AND FLOWERS (*in chorus*).

We are creatures of Bounty, throned above!
We are creatures all of His deathless love!
Winds, frosts, and flowers, His wisdom prove!
    Who shall dispute?

THE VESTALS.

DRAMATIS PERSONÆ.

JUNOA, *Vestalis Maxima.*

ANEMONE, *her Niece.*
PAX,
LIVIA,
OCTAVIA,
} *Senior Vestals.*

ZAPPI,
ILIA,
CORNELIA,
TATIA,
} *Junior Vestals.*

ATHENA, *a Greek slave.*
SLAVES IN ATTENDANCE.

THE VESTALS.

SCENE I.—*Peristylum of Numa's Palace adjoining the Temple of Vesta. Octavia, sitting with distaff and spindle. Enter* TATIA, *with a long garland of violets. Sings:*

Garlands, bay or laurel,
　For the victor's brow!
Myrtle for a bridal,
　Vervain for a vow;
Roses for the festal,
　Wreathing richly red;
Olive for the vestal,
　Parsley for the dead.*

OCTAVIA.

Ah, listless Tatia! whence comest thou?

TATIA (*throwing herself on the seat by her sister*).

From the garden, sister; there's a rose for thee,

---

* The Romans and Greeks invented a variety of crowns and appropriated them to different occasions. Those used for sacred purposes were called vervain or verbena, which could be olive, laurel, bay, oak, or parsley.

With a crystal tear-drop in its crimson heart.
Why here alone? Where are the vestals all?

          OCTAVIA.

Junoa is abroad: Anemone,
Her niece, accompanies her.

          TATIA.
                    Anemone!
She with the sensitive and tender smile,
The youngest priestess?

          OCTAVIA.
                    Yea.

          TATIA.
                    The Grecian name
Well symbolizes her too delicate
And soul-like loveliness.

          OCTAVIA.
                    And know'st thou not
As yet, our names and offices?

          TATIA.
                    Why, no!
'Twas but on the Vestalia [*] that I stood
For the first time in Vesta's *atrium*—
My small hand trembling in the Emperor's palm.[†]
To-day's the *idus*—could I know so soon?

---

[*] Principal feast of Vesta, occurring on the 9th of June.
[†] If not presented by parents, the Emperor chose the vestal by lot, and led her to the *atrium* of Vesta.

THE VESTALS.

OCTAVIA.

Ah, true! I will acquaint thee with us all.
Junoa, senior sister, titled is
Vestalis Maxima. Her thirty years
Of consecration soon expire. She then
May leave the temple, or, if she so will,
Remains in office, to instruct and rule.

TATIA.

I do not like her haughty, handsome face!

OCTAVIA.

Austere to guilt alone; thou shalt not meet
Often her peer, my Tatia; study her.
It is a soul that utterly detests
Acted as spoken falsehood—'tis a soul
Minervan in its bravery and breadth,
Its flight of intellect, its force of will.

TATIA.

Priestess of Vesta as she is, 'tis said
She doth affect the sapient goddess most.

OCTAVIA.

Blamelessly. They are twin devotions, child.
In the sacrarium, where 'tis our wont
To watch the altar's blest perpetual flame,
The dread palladium of Jove's daughter, stands
Livia and Caia Pax.*

---

* A vestal takes the prænomen "Caia," on becoming priestess.

TATIA (*laughing*).

    I know *them* well!
They are inseparable friends, and one
The other's shadow. Pax I take to be
Not over-brilliant—she is like new milk,
Fair, calm, and cool, and, if no thunder, sweet.
Livia's lithe form, and keen, inconstant eyes,
Remind me of a snake. Yet she is kind,
And gives me sweetmeats.

OCTAVIA.

    With consummate art
She can, with tongue and hand, distribute them.
O Tatia, simple Tatia! wise if young,
Canst keep a secret?

TATIA.

    Yea, thou know'st I can.

OCTAVIA.

In the first decade of thy thirty years
Thou, Ilia, Zappi, and Cornelia,
Are students, only, of our mysteries.*
A second ten gives to the vestal right
Of sacrifice and vigil at the flame
Whose perpetuity protecteth Rome.
This right is mine, and fair Anemone's;

---

* The vestals were bound by vow to thirty years' service. When chosen, they could not be less than six or more than ten years of age.

But the third decade eligible finds
The priestess for insignia of command—
The senior sister's golden wand and hoop,
The circlet of Vestales Maxima—
Should just Junoa weary of her claim,
Or Rome cry "Vale!" to her funeral urn.*

TATIA.

If this thy secret, I have naught to tell.

OCTAVIA.

Hearken, and pick the kernel from the shell.
Tullia's death leaves Livia and Pax
Aspirants for the golden hoop and wand,
Which Junoa is impatient to resign.
When in Ambition's stadium two contest,
And equally are nigh unto the goal
Of power and high position, they may wear
Without the vest of Amicitia,†
But writhing serpents lurk and war within.
Calm Pax, whose conscience hath no covert stain,
The Future Possible can coolly take,
But with a grasp of steel will hold her own
When it the Present Tangible becomes.
Livia can from Junoa hope no voice,
Yet would she climb; but in her path stands Pax,
Whom she will kiss and kiss, and from her cast.

---
* The Vestalis Maxima, after the expiration of office, might return to her family. It was, however, considered disgraceful to do so.
† Goddess of Friendship

TATIA.

O hypocrite ! But why may she not hope
Junoa's suffrage, when the Pontifex
Appoints the next Vestalis Maxima ?

OCTAVIA.

Watch, and see that which every vestal sees—
Junoa's loathing for this Livia,
Which Livia ignores, nor dare resent—
The why, she does not dare, is mystery.

TATIA.

Perhaps at her midnight vigil she hath slept,
And the sacred fire hath perished ; or she may
Have oped the awful adytum * to one
Unholy ; or she may—

OCTAVIA.

     It matters not,
My little sister, unto thee and me.

TATIA (*sighing*).

Ah, true ! I wish that we might flee away
From this vile palace and its gloomy fane.
Octavia, how I hate that stony man—
That incarnation of patrician pride,
Our father ! Was it not enough for him
That thou wast vestal ? The Lex Papia

---

* Inner part of the temple.

Forbids the Pontifex, at vacancy,
To count a vestal's sister to the score
Chosen for lottery. Suetonius bribed
Hadrian to name *me*. He would be inscribed
Sire to two vestals, since the gods denied
To such a Saturn* as he is, a son—
He'll find his Tatia missing, some fine morn.

OCTAVIA.

O foolish child ! it is impossible.
What sacrilegious hand would aid the flight
Of consecrated vestal ? Age will bring
Just estimate of each great privilege.
What ! is it naught to sit beside the throne
Of Cæsar, in the amphitheatre ?
To have the throng obsequiously give way
Before the fasces of thy retinue ?
The treaties and the testaments of kings
To hold in trust—to guard the altar-flame ;
Nay, more, that inmost adytum, the shrine
Of those most sacred relics, which are pledge
Of permanency for the sway of Rome ?

TATIA.

Sister, my soul will starve on dignity—
It must have liberty, it must have love.
Were that pale mother living, whom thy loss
Laid, broken-hearted, on the bed of death—

---

* Who, according to the fable, devoured his own children.

Wert thou not here to hold me to thine heart,
I'd leap into the fountain-vase from whence
I plucked these violets which purple thus
The glossy braidings of thy golden hair.
Octavia, thou art very beautiful!

OCTAVIA.

And very wretched, O my Tatia.

TATIA.

Why?

OCTAVIA.

'Tis my secret—one I might not tell
E'en to the winds, lest they should whisper it.
Hark, voices! Let us speak of something else.

(*Enter Junoa, Anemone, Pax, Livia, Zappi, and Cornelia. Slaves in attendance.*)

ANEMONE.

Who is the girl that, in the atrium,*
Took off thy palla, aunt? Is she a slave?

CORNELIA.

Ay! who is she? I marked her faultless face.
'Tis like a Luna's,† set in hueless stone.

---

* The vestibule of a Roman house opened into the street. The *ostium*, a wide passage, led to the *atrium*, the principal apartment. The *peristylium* was an inner court, with fountains, columns, and flowers; like the *atrium*, it was open to the sky in the center.

† Luna or Diana.

ANEMONE.

What large, grave eyes she had! What elegance
In motion or repose!

JUNOA.

Have I not told
You of Athena, my late purchase?

PAX.

Nay!

ANEMONE.

She looks of Grecian mold. From whence is she?

JUNOA.

Seat you, my sisters, and attend her tale.
Imperial Hadrian, journeying from the East,
Lingered in that Elysium of renown,
Science, and art—histrionic Attica.
Apollodorus, the famed architect,
Rejoined his master here, and here beheld
This fair Athenian girl, to bondage sold,
For crime unspecified, and advertised
A literatus.* Purchased, brought to Rome,
He found her both a bargain and a fraud.
He had but sought a draughtswoman. She proved
An artist and notarius † of the best—

---

* Literati, or literary slaves, were sold in Rome for a large sum.
† The elder Pliny, when traveling, used to take a *notarius* with him, that the slave might be ready to take down anything he wished.

Diana cold, honest, acute, but *dumb*.
Since their return, the Emperor hath had
Another quarrel with the architect,
And the old genius is, in consequence,
Sentenced to exile, and it may be death.
He strangely hath affected this dumb girl;
And, when expatriated, offered her
Her freedom; but she craved—ye marvel all!—
That he would sell or give her unto me.

OCTAVIA.

What think you of her? Doth the architect
O'errate her value?

JUNOA.

Nay: she is a pearl!
Pure as yon ray of sunlight is her soul;
And throned as loftily. Her silent lips
Are rose-red valves that close an avenue
To thought whose vistas, ever widening, wind
Columned with crystal truth, and luminous.

LIVIA.

Let's see her! Send for her!

JUNOA (*to a slave*).

Athena, here!

THE VESTALS.

(*While they await the coming of Athena, Tatia sings to a lyre.*)

TATIA.

Under the branches the green forest arches,
   Meadows lie sylvan, and mosses lie soft;
Sunlight and shadow are dancing together;
   Zephyr sits laughing and luting aloft.

Wherefore the shadow with sunlight, forever?
   Child Tatia's sunlight? 'Tis all mystery!
All things within and without are in cipher;
   Zephyr, go find, or restore me the key.

(*Speaking to herself.*)

O Arno, of mine own Etruria,
Would that I were beneath the laden vines
That shadow thy glad waves!—Athena comes!

JUNOA (*to Athena*).

The vestals fain would see and question thee.
Answer thou, on these tablets. I will read.

PAX.

Thou wast born free?

(*Athena writes on Junoa's tablets and hands them to her mistress.*)

JUNOA (*reading*).

      And though a slave, yet free.

CORNELIA (*laughing*).

That's beyond demonstration!

ATHENA (*Junoa reading for her*).

                    Rather say
That demonstration is beyond thy light.
Free am I, "by that freedom wherewith truth
Hath made me free," nor can she who wears chains,
Through her own election, wholly be a slave.

LIVIA.

For what crime wast thou unto bondage sold?

ANEMONE (*compassionately, seeing that Athena hesitates*).

Press not that question!

LIVIA.

              She *must* answer me!

JUNOA (*reading for Athena*).

There had been given to me an antique gem,
Engraven and regraven by a god.
Flawless, and formed of empyrean light.
Mine uncle, coveting its case of gold—
He did not know the jewel's priceless worth—
Bade me relinquish it; and, disobeyed,
Sold me to seize the setting.—It is his;
But the gem, the mystic jewel, still is mine.

PAX (*looking with surprise at Junoa*).

Hast seen this bauble? Slaves can not possess.

JUNOA (*answering Pax, and looking with scorn at Livia*).

She hath no gem, and Livia no reply
Even to me; upon her early past
Equivocally, vaguely, she responds.
Thus covering her reluctance to disclose
The crime, or the calamity, that brought
Her unto the catasta.* Subtle Greek,
It costs her naught to answer, and still hide
Her secret 'neath some myth or metaphor.

LIVIA (*offering her a goblet*).

Slave, pour to the penates,† and then drink.

ATHENA (*through Junoa*).

How can she pour who can not pray? For void
The sacrifice, if uninvoked the god.‡

LIVIA.

Thou'rt scarce as scrupulous on every point.
Unto what deity art vot'ress vowed?

---

* Stand in the market at which slaves were sold.
† Gods of the household.
‡ The Romans attached great importance to the form of words at prayer or sacrifice.

JUNOA.

Thus she : "All nations have their different gods
(A fact, methinks, which augurs ill to both).
Doth Livia then condemn Athena?—She
Kneels to a god unrecognized by Rome."

LIVIA.

Imperial Rome consolidates her sway
By throwing wide her temples to the gods
Of conquered realms pre-eminently thine.

JUNOA (*for Athena*).

Through Athens, once, passed a philosopher,
A citizen of Rome, and, on the hill
Of Areopagus, he, wandering, found
An altar, bearing an inscription wreathed
Within a circle : "To the unknown God."
An altar by the Academics raised
To that Eternal, Infinite, Supreme,
Whom the great sages of my native land—
Lured on by voices, faintly echoing,
Of lost and loftiest primeval truth—
Sought through dark labyrinths of uncertainty,
With Reason's *ignis fatuus* for a torch.
Athena stands before that altar now
In spirit, and to Deity unknown
She bows adoringly, invokes and pours.

LIVIA (*looking tauntingly toward Junoa*).

Monotheism! Is not this the cry
Of those impious called Christians?

      PAX (*pedantically*).
                              Not at all!
They worship three gods of beneficence,
Under the forms of water, bread, and oil.
The second, their god Messiah, was a Jew,
And apotheosized for healing skill,
Like Æsculapius. Sometimes a fourth
They add—the god of evil—whom their art
Represents satyr-like, with hoof and horn.

      JUNOA (*looking at Athena with a smile*).

Go thou, Athena, and devoutly vow
A goose to Ignorance.*
          [*To a slave, who enters with perturbed look.*
                   Well! what's amiss?

      SLAVE (*with some fragments of stone in hand*).

Caia Junoa, terrible to tell,
Some sacrilegious hand hath overthrown
The statue of great Pan. Behold the hoofs—
It is in fragments! Caia Tatia,
Who last was in the garden, perhaps can tell
The perpetrator.

---

    * An inferior deity, worshiped by the ancients.

JUNOA.

Little Tatia,
Know'st thou aught of this?

TATIA (*sullenly*).

I stoned him.

JUNOA (*with surprise*).

Thou! and why?

TATIA (*passionately*).

I will not have a god that's half a goat!

VESTALS *and* SLAVES (*in horror*).

Oh, most profane!

TATIA (*bursting into tears, impetuously*).

I have no faith in him!
He shall not be my god! He hath a tail.
When, where, and how, did he become divine?

LIVIA.

What impious freak is this? She must be whipped.

JUNOA (*looking with dislike on Livia, as she takes Tatia's hand to retire*).

Nay; time will teach her to dissemble.—Canst
Thou answer her those questions, Livia?
Thine inquisition of Athena proves
Thee much more erudite than I supposed.

When, where, and how, did Pan become a god?—
Resolve the child these questions.

    LIVIA (*bitterly*).
            Answer thou,
To their confusion, who insinuate
That, little zealous for the gods, thou art
Somewhat too hotly given to Platonize.

   JUNOA (*turning slowly around to her*).
Hast *thou* read Plato?

     LIVIA.
      Nay! the gods forbid.

     JUNOA.
He *Tatianizes* with so sure an aim,
That all Olympus trembles.
      (*Looking at her with cruel scrutiny.*)
         Hope with me
That Tullia's pallid shade return some night
To share thy temple-vigil, and disclose
These teasing problems of futurity.
       [*Exeunt all save Livia.*

LIVIA (*soliloquizing, as she paces to and fro. Zappi returns,
  and follows on tiptoe, unseen by Livia*).
 "Tullia's pallid shade!"—that *meaning* smile!
She can not know—she can not e'en suspect.

Yet is her carriage changed in my regard—
Indifference hath frozen into hate.
A lurking·fiend of mockery and scorn
Unmasks at times within her Julian eyes—
       (*Turning suddenly.*)
Methought I heard a foot-fall following me!
        (*Walking on.*)
The follies of my unforecasting days,
With sharp reproof, she ever nobly veiled.
Now somnolence at vigil—nay, far less—
Would be adjudged confinement or the lash.

 . . . .   .

We have, in common, naught; and, it may be,
That therefore grow we daily more opposed.
I can not measure her; for, mentally,
She is an ulma taller than I am.
No, nor sound her—she is deeper than my line:
With careless glance she reads me through, and I
Shrink consciously, and *this* she also sees.
We can protest when an unbidden foot
Intrudes upon our privacy of place—
Who, sanely, can protest against the glance
That forces the barred casements of the soul?

(*Zappi leaps from behind a column. Livia shrieks and cowers, covering her face with her hands.*)

     ZAPPI (*laughing*).
Thy thought is deep as slumber, Livia!

THE VESTALS.

LIVIA (*angrily*).

And dyed as darkly as her mother—Night.
Girl, thou hast frightened me, I think, to death!

ZAPPI (*still laughing*).

I fear me, Livia, thou wilt die again!
Thou thoughtest me poor Tullia! Ha! ha! ha!
I'll tell the vestals.—There! again thou'rt pale,
Wan as that white ipomea that o'erhangs
Yonder Etruscan vase. I saw thee pace
The peristylium pavement to and fro,
Murmuring unto the fount, and frowning dark
On the poor statues, odor-urns, and flowers;
Then crouched I low behind yon column's base,
To spring upon and startle thee.

LIVIA (*impatiently forcing her to a seat*).

        Sit there!
Thou giddiest vestal, and when thou hast had
Thy fill of laughter, listen unto me,
With all attention. I would ask a grace.

ZAPPI.

There! I am grave at last. What is the grace?

LIVIA.

Tell not this freak unto the vestals—say
Nothing of my alarm.

ZAPPI.
                Dost thou so fear
A little bantering?

LIVIA.
                Yea. Go lay thine hand
On Echo's golden statue, and declare
That thou wilt sacred keep my confidence,
And thou shalt know why I am thus unnerved.

(ZAPPI *lays her hand on a little statue of Echo.*)
Lo, I have promised, and am curious. Speak!

LIVIA (*after a few minutes' silence*).
Since Tullia's death, one night I watched alone
Within the temple. Gloom as deep as that
Which shrouds Avernus draped the vestibule.
Within the cella burned the sacred blaze
Unsteadily, for midnight airs astray
Stole in, with sorrowing sighs, that made me draw,
Shivering, my palla closer. Suddenly
I saw approaching, from the posticum,
A vestal in her snowy stola clad,
With her suffibulum* drawn o'er her face.

ZAPPI.
Great Jove! Who was it, Caia Livia?

---

* Head-dress of a vestal, made of fine white material bordered with purple, and secured with a clasp.

LIVIA (*with a shudder*).

'Twas Tullia.

ZAPPI.

And didst thou address her?

LIVIA.

Yea!

ZAPPI.

What said she?

LIVIA.

Almost senseless—horrified,
I could not catch the purport of her words,
Whose hollow whisper came as from afar.
Zappi, for reasons twain do I impart
This secret to thee: Firstly, let it buy
Thy silence on my terror. Secondly,
That thou mayst be induced sometimes to share
My nightly vigils. Vestal, thou shalt find
That Livia's gratitude is Zappi's gold.

ZAPPI (*carelessly*).

Call on me when thou wilt. I watch unfeed
All the more readily, that I incline
To think that fancy played the fool with thee.
It was Junoa. Tullia and she
Had the same height and dignity of port.

LIVIA.

Preposterous, Zappi! Dost thou think I slept?

VESTALS.

ZAPPI.

Nay ; but I think Junoa did. She walks
More frequently of late than was her wont.

LIVIA.

"Walks!" in her sleep? Junoa somnambulist?

ZAPPI.

Pretend not ignorance. Thou knowest it.

LIVIA (*rising and clasping her hands*).
I did not !

ZAPPI.

Well ! e'en so, why thus perturbed ?

LIVIA.

The memory of that apparition moves
Me ever thus. Leave me awhile alone ;
And may the fate of Echo be thine own,
If thou betray the trust reposed in thee !

[*Exit Zappi*

Junoa !—I could swear 'twas Tullia !
And yet it may have been. Gods ! If awake,
She hath my secret ; for in wild affright
I craved her mercy . . . . Nay ! 'twas Tullia,
Languid and dreamy, as she was ere death.
Junoa's soul would emanate in sleep—
Junoa !—and awake !—Ay ! 'twould explain

Her altered bearing. O dread Nemesis!
Is this of thy ordaining? Air! more air!—
This place is close!—Junoa? . . . Tullia?

SCENE II.—*Numa's Palace by moonlight. Enter* ATHENA,
with a lyre. She advances, murmuring to herself:

O Night! of dreams, of sleep, of shadowy death!
Mysterious mother, blest by thy cool breath,
   Athena wanders free.
Soft, O ye winds! Bid not the waves complain.
Hush, whispering olives! ye will wake again
   Godless captivity.

Dropping her lyre, and leaning on a pedestal, she soliloquizes:

Tearless, O Ion! though yon argent moon
 Queening the azure of Italia's sky,
Illumes *thee*, O thou realm of old renown—
 Of heroes, poets, sages—not to die,
Thou realm supreme, save for an Orient land
Blest in each blade of grass, each grain of sand.

Tearless, though memory paints a maiden lost
 Midst myriads on an Acropolian flight
Upsweeping—an interminable host—
 Priests, warriors, victims, in the rich sunlight
The past all present, and the maiden's cheek
Robes pride in crimson—she is Attic—Greek.

Tearless, O Ion, though Ausonia's* chains
  Weigh heavily on hands, and heart, and soul,
And midst the throngs that fill her streets and fanes,
  There's not a face to solace or console.
And yet, O Lord! Love strengthens in the strife:
Thou givest life and love—take love and life.

Taking her lyre, she sings as the moon rises:

  Rise without peer, O Queen!.
    O virgin, crowned!
  Illimitable space—illumed—serene,
  Thrills, as on high empyreal lyres gleam,
    Thy praise to sound.

  The breath of seraphim
    Bears up thy throne;
  Light inaccessible receives it in;
  Thy lilied feet press down the coils of sin—
    Shield me, thine own!

Enter Anemone, timidly. She pauses, looks around fearfully, and then approaches Athena.

ANEMONE.

I heard thy lyre, and low, sweet song afar,
And through the grove's funereal shadows passed,
Half breathless, love, to meet thee.

---

* The Italian peninsula, lying west of Greece, was called by the Greeks Hesperia, and by poetical writers Ausonia.

ATHENA.
Is it late?

ANEMONE.
'Tis midnight, but I dared not come before :
Pax vigil keeps to-night. I took her watch;
Then fled, and left the evil-one to trim
The brazier for himself. (*Starting.*) Soft! What is that?

ATHENA.
A Ceres, that in moonlit marble weeps
Lest Proserpine— Why dost thou tremble so?

ANEMONE.
Oh, I am like a fawn that, from the hounds,
Hides, startling, in some arborescent wild.
Athena, I have never seen thee fear!

ATHENA (*throwing her arm about her protectingly*).
Fear now, Anemone, can move my heart
But through affection. I intensely fear
The loss, through sin, of His complacency
With whom interiorly I walk. I fear
When peril threatens my beloved—but here,
It sweeps, alone, the surface of my soul;
For, 'thwart the storm-cloud, falls that strong, bright ray,
The fiat of Omniscient, pitying Love.
This garden scene is lovely!

ANEMONE.

                Yea, Queen Night
Sweeps it, bedecked in diamonds, the sole gem
On her rich robe of velvet shadowing.
They flash from out the fount; they look on me
From the large stars, grown pensive with late watch.
Thine eyes, beloved, from gazing much thereon,
Have caught their earnest glance of holy calm.
They dust the dewy sward with brilliancy,
They glisten on the satin-surfaced leaves,
That whisper low together with delight,
As Zephyr, Night's fan-bearer, wanders down
The clustered pillars of yon portico,
Which breaks, in silvery bars, the clear moonlight.
Soon will the pale lights of the orient gleam.
Give thou my pagan soul supernal light:
Sum to me, sister, all that thou hast taught,
And I will ponder till we meet again.

ATHENA (*raising her hand to heaven*).

One dread, eternal God, Anemone,
In act and essence one—in persons three—
Infinity, Omniscience, Justice, Love,
Author of all, beneath, around, above.
Love would have love—angels and man were made;
Love must be free—angels and mortals strayed;
Mercy and Love embraced—the Word assumed,
Man was redeemed, exalted, and replumed;

And his rebellion canceled in the tide
Of Him who not alone assumed, but died.

ANEMONE.

Who comes? Great God! it is Junoa! Fly!

ATHENA (*drawing Anemone into the shadow of the shrubbery*).

She searches for us! Fly, Anemone!
A vestal may not be abroad at night.
Thou art without the limits. I am safe.

ANEMONE.

She dare not search *alone* at this late hour.
Yea—see!—she is asleep. Her long dark locks
Flow loose above her stola, and thou know'st
That vestals may not wear their hair unbound.
When mentally disturbed it is her wont,
Thus to walk sleeping. See! she bears a scroll.

ATHENA.

The Gospel. I this morning left the book
Upon her toilet.

Enter Livia, who cautiously follows Junoa, throws down a suffibulum on the path, and disappears.

Livia! thou art lost!
She goes, yet may return. O vestal, fly!

ANEMONE.

Ah, look, Athena! My poor aunt hath turned
Direct unto Egena's Fount—she'll drown!
Alas! she'll drown!

ATHENA.

    Leave her to me, and go!
I do not fear her wrath. 'Tis said I am
A favorite with Vestales Maxima. [*Exit Anemone.*

(*Taking Junoa's hand:*)

Caia Junoa, where wanderest thou? Awake!

JUNOA.

Abroad at night! Athena, where are we?

ATHENA.

Beside Egena's Fountain—I knew not
Thou wast somnambulist. This ne'er again
Shall happen while I serve thee.

JUNOA (*lays her hand on Athena's arm with surprise*).
Thou speakest!—and wert dumb, or feigned to be.

ATHENA.

I feigned.

JUNOA.

   And why, Athena, this deceit?
Have I so dealt with thee?—I, who have given
Thee confidence, yea, love, and thou a slave?

ATHENA.

My chains, Junoa, prove no less a love.

JUNOA.

To know thee is to know thou doest naught
Without just reason. Why these bonds *for me ?*

ATHENA.

I am of Attica. My father was
Archon in Athens, and, at death, bequeathed
A large estate unto his only child,
Whom he committed to a brother's care.
That brother, false and avaricious, loved
His niece too little and her gold too well ;
And 'neath a feline fawning watched the time
Wherein to leap upon his last akin.
Not long he waited : he was truly told
That she was Christian—sometime proselyte
Of blest Quadratus, bishop, saint, and sage.
How zealous grew he for the gods of Greece !
Accused, condemned, defrauded, sold a slave,
I was, by Apollodorus, brought to Rome :
Feigning a dumbness that might me defend
From invocation of false deity,
And unto me insure a service long
'Neath this hot-headed but most kind old man,
With whom a knowledge of my vocal gift
Might have been an incitement to consign
The songstress to less conscientious care.

My God had left me nothing but Himself;
I vowed that I would nothing have but Him.
My life a lowly-veiled apostleship—
My death, His glory in red martyrdom.
We met, Junoa, at the architect's;
I saw in thee an upright soul, that lacked
Light only, and for Christ did covet thee.

JUNOA.

Oft have I heard that Christians would o'erturn
The Pennine Alps to make a proselyte.
Here is an instance. Now mark, Athena, well—
Enthusiast, enigma, that thou art—
Although in Rome's plurality of gods
My faith be brittle, mine integrity,
Mine honor pledged in mine important trust,
Is as Olympus. I already have
A copy of the Hebrew Pentateuch,
Sent me by Julius Severus; and know
Much of the subtile speculations born
Of thy bright land, which give, in sound sublime,
A chord of intellectual harmony—
But of this matter we will speak anon.
Tamper not with the vestals. Disobey,
And thou, despite my love, shalt know the lash!

ATHENA.

Lo! bright the morning breaks!

####### JUNOA.

> We must retire.

(Picking up a suffibulum.)

A suffibulum here in the garden! Strange!

####### ATHENA.

A vestal, perhaps, hath passed here recently.

####### JUNOA (*quickly*).

Not in suffibulum.* It can be worn
Only at sacrifice. Go, summon all.
> [*Enter vestals, wearing suffibulums.*

Ye look surprised—an early summons, true.
I have been sleep-walking, and, by this fount,
Found this suffibulum. Pray, whose is it?

####### PAX.

Mine is mislaid.

####### LIVIA.

And yet it was thy turn to watch last night.

####### PAX.

I had a headache, and Anemone
Offered to take my vigil.

---

* A vestal could not wear her hair flowing. It was either braided or bound close to the head by the white woolen *vitta*, which was a roll of snowy wool, hanging in long, broad ribbons behind.

ANEMONE.
So I did.

LIVIA (*laughing*).
Now, Pax, confess! Thou thoughtest midnight air
A specific.

PAX (*reprovingly*).
This is no case for mirth;
I went unto my couch.

JUNOA.
Go, search again.
Each vestal hath but one suffibulum,
That only in the temple can be worn.—
Canst thou remember having thine, Caia Pax,
Last evening?

PAX.
Yea; thy niece assisted me
To fold it on returning.

LIVIA.
Howsoe'er
Came this suffibulum unto the walk,
'Tis thine, O Pax. See! here I marked thy name.

PAX.
Why! yes, 'tis mine. But how did it come here?

LIVIA.

A secret, Pax, that only thou canst solve.

PAX (*indignantly*).

What! Dost *thou*, Livia—thou, my friend avowed—
Harbor suspicions that dishonor me?

LIVIA.

And canst thou blame me? Saidst thou not to me,
As o'er the balcony we leaned last eve:
"The garden hath its secrets, Livia—
What though its ilex and its olive groves
Are tireless whisperers, they can tell no tales
Of stolen rendezvous and sweet starlight"?

PAX (*passionately*).

'Tis false, thou sycophant! I said to thee:
"The garden hath its secrets, Livia—
These orange-trees gave promise of much fruit;
I think 'tis stolen by the slaves at night."

JUNOA.

Silence, Caia Livia!

TATIA.

   I think 'tis time;
She is not *yet* Vestalis Maxima.

ATHENA.

Caia Livia that suffibulum threw here.

LIVIA.

Thou liest, slave!

(*All the vestals, except Junoa, look toward Athena with astonishment.*)

ILIA *and* ZAPPI.

Athena speaks!

OCTAVIA (*to Junoa*).

She spoke!

TATIA (*to Junoa*).

The Greek, Junoa, spoke!

CORNELIA.

How! Thou wert dumb.

ATHENA.

To serve myself, and vocal to serve Pax.
Within this garden I have passed the night.
An hour ere dawn, down to the fountain came
Caia Junoa, in her sleep astray.
Behind her, cautiously, Caia Livia stole,
And that suffibulum threw on the path.

JUNOA (*after a general silence*).

Caia Livia, speak!

VESTALS.

Disgraceful!

OTHERS OF THE VESTALS.

                                Livia, shame!

CORNELIA.

Disinterested friendship! That is all.
Caia Livia, o'er-solicitous for Pax,
Threw that suffibulum, to ward from her
Impending dangers, veiled in dignities.

           LIVIA (*looking around boldly*).

Shocked into silence, vestals? Speechless?

                  JUNOA.

                                      Nay!
Exonerate thyself, if so thou canst.

                  LIVIA.

Aversion for my person must have dulled
Your better judgment, vestals. Do you dare
Vituperate a sister, on the charge—
The accusation of a brazen slave?   [*To Athena.*
Thou insignificant and servile worm,
Accusest thou a vestal—and the niece
Of the proconsul Aulus Fabius?
I'll have thee for thy falsehood flayed alive!

           ANEMONE (*hastily*).

Thou shalt not harm her. I was also here,
And saw thee throw the veil before mine aunt.

THE VESTALS.

JUNOA (*startled*).

Thou here, Anemone? Thou here at night!

ANEMONE.

I knew Athena had the faculty
Of speech, and followed, to converse with her.

LIVIA (*mockingly*).

Thou hadst best look to this most erudite,
Most virtuous slave, Junoa. I suspect
She's of the sect of Eleutherius.*
It seems Anemone can make a slip
As well as Livia. If Pax were sick,
And thy fair niece abroad with this bold slave,
Who fed the sacred flame, I fain would ask?

JUNOA.

True, Livia! I will look to it. Retire,
Most noble ladies. I would speak alone
With Caia Anemone.—Athena, stay!

[*Exeunt all, except Anemone and Athena.*

Niece, hast thou lost thy reason? Freaks like this
Cloud the clear crystal of a vestal's fame.
Why hast thou left thyself in Livia's power?

ANEMONE (*speaking to herself*).

Hath not my soul been ever to her ken
As limpid waters? Shall I now conceal

---

* A Roman youth of consular rank, consecrated by Pope Anaclete for the see of Aquileia, at the age of twenty, martyred by Hadrian.

When the glad sunrise of electing grace
Fills it with fecund and refulgent light?
Junoa, I am Christian; and will die,
Rather than by lustrations—sacrifice,
Deny in deed what I in soul revere!

JUNOA (*threateningly to Athena*).
This is thy work, and thou hast done it well.

ATHENA.

It is the Spirit's! Blessed be He who used
So faulty and so weak an instrument!

JUNOA.

And ye, with Christian stubbornness, will hold
This mad impiety unto the death?

BOTH.
       We shall.

JUNOA.

Oh, would that Tiber, lapsing cold and gray
'Neath morn's chill mantle, were my sepulchre!
By these new phantasies, steeled and possessed,
Ye care not how ye trample on my heart.

(*To her niece.*)

And thou—a moment since I chafed to think
An indiscretion might attaint thy name;
Now black dishonor, specter-like, appalls—

THE VESTALS.

Thy public death, and my attending shame!
And yet I die not. O Anemone!
Think of our ancient and illustrious line.
Must I be thine accuser, or make void
Mine oath to Hadrian? How will Rome exclaim!
Speak to me, niece! speak! Art thou ice or stone?

ATHENA.

Stand, as the mountain pine unto the storm,
O flower of the zephyr! I can see,
Above thy head, red-scarred and radiant Hands
Holding the virgin-martyrs' palm and crown.

JUNOA.

Heartless, ungrateful girl! Why have I let
The moonbeam loveliness of that chill face
Work in my heart unwonted sorcery?
Could I but kill the love that bleedeth here,
I'd crush thee out of life! Go hence! Begone!
I am not bound by oath in thy regard.

ATHENA.

"Heartless," Junoa! "Thankless!" Soul beloved,
For whose salvation I have vowed my life;
Let Reason reascendant plead for me.
Touching Anemone, bethink thyself,
Thine oath compels thee to divulge alone
Those violations of Pompilius'* law

---

* Numa Pompilius.

That bear relation to the vestal vow.
But *she* whom Hadrian shall interrogate
On her infraction of nocturnal rules,
May give the reason wherefor, and disclose
Who her instructress and companion was—
And thus concede to me one half her crown.

(*Enter Octavia and Tatia hastily.*)

TATIA.

Pray, pardon this intrusion!

JUNOA (*absently*).

Enter, child.

TATIA.

I fear me that Caia Livia hath sent
Note of this trouble to the Emperor.

ANEMONE.

Great God! so soon?

ATHENA.

Love speed the wings of time.

(*Enter Livia, followed by Pax, Zappi, Cornelia, and Ilia.*)

LIVIA.

Are we at liberty to enter?

JUNOA (*vacantly*).

Yea.

THE VESTALS.

LIVIA (*excitedly*).

I wish the vestals, all, to understand
That I have written to the Emperor.
As Pontifex, it is his right to know
That Christian slaves are harbored in the fane
Of Vesta, and that one hath dared to draw
A priestess from her duty. That I have
Suspected this, and to assure myself
Did, last night, violate nocturnal law.

OCTAVIA (*reproachfully*).

'Twas Zappi that advised her so to do.

ZAPPI.

Livia is mine agnatus.* Nor do I
Deny the sympathy I feel for her :
She showed to me her tablets, and disclosed
Her intent to apprise the Pontifex,
Saying Junoa might not dare suppress
A fault so flagrant, and her niece concerned—
And I agreed ; for it is just that she
Defend herself, since she must be accused.

JUNOA (*with a scornful look at Livia*).

Under the cover of religious zeal,
A last despairing leap for this poor toy.
(*Breaks the golden wand, and throws it to the floor.*)

---
* Relation on the father's side.

O wily woman—meshed in thine own net,
Thou hast o'erreached thyself and ruined all.
Hadrian in his Tivolian villa stays.
He will be here anon, and when he comes
Defend thyself, O harpy, if thou canst !—
I charge thee with the death of Tullia !

LIVIA (*tossing her arms in the air*).
'Tis false ! 'tis false ! I call on all the gods !

JUNOA.

On the whole Pantheon, if so thou please.
Hark ! I will prove it.—Hither, Ilia.

ILIA.

Ere Tullia's death, a marked estrangement grew
Betwixt herself and Livia. Hear the cause :
One eve, to Tullia's couch of wasting pain
Old Poppo came, her freedwoman and nurse.
Saith Poppo : " These are splendid nectarines.
Whose gift are they ?—a present from thy friend
The vestal Livia ? " Saith Tullia : " Yea.
I wonder are they wholesome ? " Poppo then :
" Thy little slave Chrysanthus lieth sick,
With all thy symptoms, and he still insists
Thy nectarines (oft thieved by him) the cause."
Then languid Tullia looked in Poppo's eyes,
And Poppo sat and looked her back again,
Till from the terrace Caia Tullia called :

"Come, Argus! Argus!" and the peacock came.
"Feed Argus daily with my nectarines."
"And if he dieth," Poppo asked, "what then?"
But Tullia answered not—and Argus died.
When Tullia's death drew nigh, she did depose
That which I fear to say—Junoa can,
As witness, to this story's truth attest.

LIVIA.

A plot! I dare ye, prove it!

JUNOA.

                    Vestal, more!
'Twas night, and Livia's vigil. Suddenly,
Nigh to the sacred adytum, there stood
The ghost of Tullia, so Livia thought.
Shrieking with terror, at its feet she fell
Abject, confessed her crime, and mercy craved:
A ghost in fact—but clad in clay—myself.
Awakened by the scream that I had caused,
Livia did sign, at my command, a writ
Which briefly gives confession to her guilt.

LIVIA (*sinking at Junoa's feet, and clinging to her stola*).

Junoa, pity. I am guilty! Spare!
I aimed at Pax alone.

JUNOA.

             And, missing her,
Would strike Junoa through her niece and slave.
Unhand my stola!

LIVIA.

Let my tears entreat!

JUNOA.

In vain they flow. Is not this work thine own?
And from Pandora's box e'en Hope is flown.

SCENE III.—*Arena of the Coliseum. Enter Athena, leading Anemone by the hand.*

ATHENA (*looking around*).

The Amphitheatre! Redeemer, strength!

ANEMONE.

Where are the lions?

ATHENA.

Not as yet set free.

ANEMONE (*shrinking, and drawing her veil around her*).

Ah! would that I could hide! A million eyes
Are on us, darling.

ATHENA.

Pray, Anemone.

ANEMONE.

It thunders!

ATHENA.

Nay; Rome rises to salute
The Emperor.

ANEMONE.

What did that lictor say?

ATHENA.

That to the podium we must nearer stand,
That Hadrian may question if he choose;
That, should the lions lead us to abjure,
We need but raise an arm.

ANEMONE.

I never will!
Ah, Heart of Christ! The lions!

ATHENA (*clasping her hands*).

Jesus, strength!

ANEMONE.

If I should raise mine arm—

ATHENA.

I'll keep it down.

ANEMONE (*throwing her arms around Athena in terror*).

Oh, throw thine arms around me! Clasp me close
To thy strong heart. They come! Athena, see!
How that great monster boundeth o'er the sands,
Lashing his tawny sides with angry tail—
His eyes like lurid fire-balls!

ATHENA.

Sister, pray!

ANEMONE.

There is another!—and a third! My God,
They shake the Coliseum with their roar!
I faint, Athena!

ATHENA (*looking up to heaven*).
O Maria, aid!

ANEMONE (*suddenly standing erect, sings*).
Oh, Thou art beautiful, my Love!
  Thine arms invite—what holds me here?
A million sunbursts break above,
  Seraphic forms are floating near.
My God, my Love!
  Is death then past? Why did I fear?

ATHENA (*looking earnestly at Anemone*).
She is in ecstasy. Love, singest thou?

ANEMONE.

Oh, yes, Athena!—join me—all is o'er!
The angels bear us on their gleaming wings,
And midst them sits our little Tatia.
I gaze on the Man-God—He smiles; my soul
Upsoars, all lost in an exquisite bliss!

(*Enter Junoa. She stands beside Athena.*)

JUNOA.

Athena, I am with thee.

ATHENA (*without turning*).

                That should be
The voice of dear Junoa. Wherefore here?

JUNOA.

To die with thee. I have declared myself
A Christian.

ANEMONE (*turning to Junoa with a smile*).

                Aunt, thy face is glorified—
Haloed with radiance, as Athena's is! (*Sings.*)

> *Lead us, ye Lilies, to the Lamb;*
>   *Intone the martyrs' joyous hymn;*
> *Tell Him, unworthy as I am,*
>   *I gave my life for love of Him—*
>   *But painless gave;*
> *He veils in bliss Death's visage grim.*

A VOICE (*from the audience*).

Caia Junoa, 'tis the Emperor's will
That thou make known the causes that have led
Thee to abandon the immortal gods.

JUNOA.

Couch there, ye monster ministers of death—
Held by the angry angel of Rome's Church,
While I speak truth unto its pagan lord!
Why hath Junoa renounced the gods of Rome?
Asks Hadrian this? He hath been told before;

But, since he wills it, once more ere she dies:
Because the vain imaginings and myths
Which Homer sang, for pleasure or for fame,

Shall find her doubtful, credulous no more;
Because, within her, hath been ever that
Which loathed all moral foulness; which aspired
To beauty, purity, and truth supreme;
Which craved a higher good than earth could give;
Which cried a deep "Amen!" when Reason asked
A loftier Deity than thought could frame—
Her own frail nature easily excel;
Because, in fine, the calm sunrise of grace
Illumes her heart, which, like the Theban* stone,
Gives sweet response, in strain of breaking strings.
Hadrian asks "Why?" who in his secret soul,
And midst his literati, loves to scoff
Rome's time-worn superstitions! Hadrian asks,
Whose temples, statueless and incomplete,
So oft erected, and as often razed,
Have left the mob to marvel at the moods
Of Rome's immutable! How should it know
That the apologists of Christian truth
Have held to him the scale of destiny—
Have weighed against the martyr's gory vest
The purple toga by a Cæsar worn?
Hadrian dares not that which Junoa dares;
She dares not that which yet he shall—despair!
O souls, souls, souls, that circle to the skies—
Senators, equites, and plebeians—

---

* The gigantic statue of Memnon in Thebes, said to give to the first rays of sunrise a sound like the breaking of harp-strings.

The God Creator bowed Himself to earth,
Incarnate died upon the cross for you!
Who shall convince you, O philosophers,
Who look on me, suspicion and disdain
Glittering steel-clad and cold within your eyes?
Against eternal light ye turn the light
Which it bestows, and would with Lucifer
Exalt self-blatant, even to the sun.
Who will convince you, O luxurious!
Souls that might sail, but for the pampered clay
Ignobly dragging anchor midst the drift,
While sweep the vigorous on to victory;
Who turn in prayerless and unhumble scorn
From the soul's voiceless groping, questioning,
To seek in pleasure's cup a Lethean wine.
Ah! who will give you liberty and light,
You hordes of ignorance, you sons of toil?
Whom Rome, the "wondrous, terrible, and strong,
Down-treads, and tears with iron tooth and heel." *
The Crucified! The Future opes to me—
I see His ensign, still triumphant, lead
O'er falling thrones, red fields, and slow decline.
Crumble thou, Rome of clay!—thou art of time:
Then from thine ashes, phœnix-like, arise
Resplendent, and to last unto the End.

---

* "And after this, I beheld, in the vision of the night, and lo! a fourth beast, terrible, wonderful, and exceedingly strong: it had great iron teeth, eating and breaking in pieces, and treading down the rest with its feet."—DANIEL, chap. vii.

Up, noble beasts, and spring!—My soul doth pant,
Impatient to be free. Great Michael, grant
Me victory!—The lions—Lord, I wait!
Knowing I love Thee! But how late! how late!
                    [*Dies by the lions.*

LITTLE TIPTOE.

CHARACTERS.

DAME MARGUERITE.
LITTLE TIPTOE, *her niece.*
THE PRÉVÔT OF PUY-DE-DÔME.
ANGÉLIQUE, } *servants to Dame Marguerite.*
BETTINE,
FAIRY QUEEN, AND ATTENDANT FAIRIES.

LITTLE TIPTOE.

SCENE I.—*The Sylvan Dell.   Enter Little Tiptoe.*

TIPTOE.

'Tis midnight!—twelve, by yonder silver moon;
The monastery chimes will ring it soon;
And, at the last long-drawn and solemn stroke,
This glen will fill with all the fairy folk.
My auntie says I should not love so well
The merry elves that haunt her Sylvan Dell;
Shall watch their merry masquerade no more—
Their frolic on the river's reedy shore.
To fly from them, how much soe'er they seek,
I purpose oft; but, ah! the flesh is weak.
Last night I woke, and they were underneath
My bowery lattice where the woodbines wreathe.
I knew it by their laughter, light and low;
By fire-flies passing, goldenly aglow.
I heard them call me, "Tiptoe, come and dance!"
And through the diamond panes I saw them glance.
Hark! the first stroke of twelve tolls out the bell;
I'll dance *once* more—then, fairies all, farewell!

(*Chimes ring. Fairies enter, dancing. The Queen takes Tiptoe by the hand. She dances with them. Enter Dame Marguerite.*)

DAME MARGUERITE.

Good gracious! Marvelous! The fairy-folk!
Of whom my Tiptoe hath so often spoke;
I've thought it but the dreams that fancy fill,
When she, at morning rising, wearied still,
Would crave more slumber, urging that she danced
One half the night whene'er the fairies chanced
To call her. (*Calling.*) Tiptoe! Tiptoe! As I live,
I'll punish thee!

TIPTOE (*coming forward*).

O dearest aunt, forgive!
No more I'll disobey.

AUNT.

Thou naughty one!
What have these wretched little creatures done
To witch you so?

FAIRY QUEEN.

Be civil, dame! Take care!

DAME MARGUERITE.

Thou threaten'st *me*, thou little mite!—I dare
The worst that thou canst do. This Sylvan Dell

Is *mine*, thou atom—understand me *well!*
Gypsies, or beggars, tinkers, tramps, or elves,
Shall ne'er, if I can help, here camp themselves.

FIRST FAIRY (*reproachfully*).

Class *us* with "gypsies," dame?—How impolite!

DAME.

They're human beings, at least, thou graceless sprite!

SECOND FAIRY.

With "beggars," dame?—We never asked of *thee*.

DAME.

With thieves—that's worse! ye steal my niece from me.

THIRD FAIRY.

With "tinkers," dame?—We never mend a pot.

DAME.

Not that much thrift among ye—lazy lot!

FOURTH FAIRY.

And, dame, we never *tramp;* for we have wings
To help our heels.

DAME.

    Ye scoffing, mocking things!
I'll get a broom and sweep ye off the grass.
This Sylvan Dell is mine—ye shall not pass

Through it, *ma foi!* I've said it! who shall dare
To contradict? It never more shall bear
The title "Dell" or "Sylvan." I'll put round
Placards: "Beware! Dame Marguerite's Bleaching-Ground."

FAIRY QUEEN (*laughing*).

Oh, never!—"Bleaching-Ground!"—'twould lose its spell.
'Twas ever ours—is ours—*our* "Sylvan Dell."

FAIRIES (*singing*).

Sylvan Dell! Sylvan Dell!
Farewell, Tiptoe! Little Tiptoe. [*They begin to retire.*

QUEEN.

Airy, graceful, lovely Tiptoe!

TIPTOE (*singing*).

Merry fairies—loving fairies.

ALL.

Fare-thee-well! Oh, fare-thee-well! [*Exeunt all.*

SCENE II.—*Enter Dame Marguerite, leading Tiptoe, and followed by Angélique and Bettine, carrying a basket.*

ANGÉLIQUE.

Where's the sheets?

TIPTOE.

     O Angélique, look there!
They're on the lindens, fluttering in the air.

DAME.

Angélique, did you dare climb those trees?
And hang those sheets where every passing breeze
Might rend them?

ANGÉLIQUE.

     Madame Marguerite, on my word,
I blush for you. A question *so absurd!*

BETTINE.

Where's all Dame Marguerite's ruffs of finest lace?

ANGÉLIQUE.

I see them! O good Heavens! what a place!
Into the heart of those thick brambles drawn,
Ne'er to be got, unless in pieces torn.

DAME.

The gowns, the caps, the aprons! there are none!

TIPTOE.

Ha! ha! ha! O auntie dear! What fun!
Your effigy, and Bettine's, in the brook;
There's Angélique—stiff, stuffed with grasses—look!

DAME.

Ma foi! I'm speechless! The audacity!—
Tiptoe, Bettine, Angélique, all ye three
Sit silent there; sit silent, and sit still—
I'll prosecute these fairies, that I will!
I'm going for the Prévôt. Do not fear;
Although he's stout, I'll have him quickly here.

(*They sit in silence. Angélique and Bettine fall slowly asleep. While they nod, two or three little fairies steal in and kiss Tiptoe. Enter Prévôt (a pompous-looking little man), with Dame Marguerite.*)

PRÉVÔT.

Ladies, the great felicity is mine
Of wishing you good-morning. What a fine
Day we are going to have!—Ah, mademoiselle!
        (*To Tiptoe.*)
What tales are these that your good aunt doth tell?

DAME (*crossly*).

Sit on that stump, monsieur, immediately,
And get to business.

PRÉVÔT.

    Madame, pardon me—
But did I hear aright? Doth it become
My dignity—I, Prévôt of Puy-de-Dôme—
To dispense justice from a stump? You joke!

DAME.

Oh, the importance of great *little* folk!
Am I not sitting on a stone, monsieur?

PRÉVÔT.

Pardon, madame! I saw not! True—you are.
Where the defendants in this case unique?
Of course, they would not dare to harm or trick
A prévôt!

DAME.

Tiptoe, summon them, *at once;*
And don't sit staring, like a pompous dunce!

TIPTOE, *advancing to the front of the stage, sings.**

ELVES OF THE WILDWOOD.

Elves of the wildwood,
Where wander ye now?
I'm calling, I'm calling. If hidden are ye,
From green sunlit forest, from bare mountain-brow,
Come luting, come laughing, come loving to me.
'Tis Tiptoe, your Tiptoe, that calls.

FAIRIES.

We come, for 'tis Tiptoe that calls.

TIPTOE.

'Tis Tiptoe, your Tiptoe, that calls.

---

* To the air of "Entends-tu?" by Tito Mattei.

FAIRIES.

We come, from our caverns and halls,
Neath heathery hill-tops and wild water-falls.

(*Enter Fairy Queen, followed by attendant fairies. They sing.*)

DANCE OF THE FAIRIES.

Dance, ye elves, to chiming bells;
   Trip it lightly, as ye come;
Blow your pink-lipped ocean-shells;
   Dance ye merrily, every one.

Flowery festoons intertwine,
   Floating robes of red fox-glove;
In a merry march combine,
   Toss your bluebell-caps above.

Dance, ye fairies, with the birds;
   Dance ye with the waves, the breeze;
Dance ye where the gnat-fly herds,
   Dance ye with the poplar-leaves.

(*Fairies range themselves before the Prévôt, who runs away, but is brought back by Dame Marguerite and Angélique.*)

PRÉVÔT (*to the fairies, looking very much alarmed*).
Mesdames, messieurs, Dame Marguerite, whom I hold
To be a person of no common mold—

FAIRIES (*laughing*).
Well done, good Prévôt! That she *is*. Go on!
We hold, she might be less the Amazon.

PRÉVÔT.

Hath represented unto me that you,
In spite of placards, pasted up to view—
Of spring-locks, man-traps, bull-dogs, that abound—
Will trespass on her field, called "Bleaching-Ground"—

FAIRIES.

"Bleaching-Ground!"   Not at all—'tis "Sylvan Dell."

PRÉVÔT.

Oh, very well, good fairies, very well!
But, as this field is hers (as you can find—
She holds the deeds, all duly sealed and signed),
If she can prove that you have, in the night,
Here entered, and done damage, in despite
Of law and order—why! 'tis plain to you—

FAIRIES (*laughing*).

Go on, good Prévôt; pray, what will you do?
Ha! ha! ha! ha!   Pray, what will you do?

PRÉVÔT (*taking snuff elaborately*).

If, I repeat, the aforesaid worthy dame—
In common parlance Marguerite called, the same
Being Madame Javotte—proves what she has advanced,
And that ye have, despite her, nightly danced—

FAIRIES (*dancing*).

Have danced, do dance, shall dance, good Prévôt—well?

PRÉVÔT (*sternly*).
I'll fine you all for forcing Sylvan Dell!

FAIRY QUEEN (*sings*).
Where brightest beams the moon?

FAIRIES.
Over the Sylvan Dell.

QUEEN.
Where fairest night-flowers bloom?

FAIRIES.
Down in the Sylvan Dell.

QUEEN.
Where do the zephyrs sigh
Sweetest their lullaby?
Where stillest starlights lie?

FAIRIES.
Over the Sylvan Dell, the Sylvan Dell.

(*Fairies begin to dance, and while dancing pelt the Prévôt with flowers. He turns to run away.*)

DAME.
Ma foi! what cowardice! Angélique, Bettine,
Hold ye the silly wight your hands between.

I will unto the Seigneur take my case,
Unless he fine them, ere we leave this place.

QUEEN.

The good man wastes his time, tenacious dame;
You, yours of greater worth. We fairies claim
This Sylvan Dell. Dare not that claim dispute!
When the Great Lawgiver did institute
The first sign of the seven, this beauteous spot,
With many others, fell unto our lot:
And we will hold it, dancing here at night,
Up the long ladders of the moonbeams bright;
Lurking at day, or sleeping out its hours,
Pillowed upon the pollen of the flowers.
Woe to that mortal that shall hold her own
That realm wherein I rear my fairy throne!
Her health shall fail, as rills the summer rain;
Her gold shall fail, as waxen tapers wane;
Let her beware! nor herb, nor brute, nor man
Can prosper where the Elf-Queen breathes her ban.

TIPTOE.

O my own aunt, who ever unto me
Hath been so stern yet loving, patiently
Hear my suggestions.—O ye fairies gay,
My merry, only playmates many a day,
Hear Little Tiptoe, by her word abide;
For love of her, let her your cause decide.

FAIRIES (*singing*).

Speak! sweet Tiptoe—
Little Tiptoe!
Airy, graceful, lovely Tiptoe.

DAME.

Speak, child—I give this Sylvan Dell to thee.
Let go the Prévôt, Angélique, and see
He gets his breakfast. "Love" indeed, the elf!
My niece, at least, belongs unto myself.

TIPTOE.

Let Sylvan Dell be *thine*, dear aunt, by day,
Your snowy linen o'er the sward to lay—
Let Sylvan Dell be *yours*, dear elves, at night,
To hold your revels by the glow-worm's light.

DAME.

Agreed!—I'm just as hungry as a bear!
Fairies, will you a cup of coffee share?

FAIRY QUEEN.

We will, dear dame, and bring it to the Dell,
Which I will bless with many a fairy spell.
Here shall the ripest fruits tempt hand and lip;
Here shall rare game abound, rich honey drip;
The mushroom grow abundant in the grass,
The sweetest airs and clearest waters pass;

And veins of metal, beds of gems beneath,
We to our favorite Tiptoe do bequeath.
   Farewell, Tiptoe!
   Little Tiptoe!
   Airy, graceful, lovely Tiptoe!
   Fare-thee-well! Oh, fare-thee-well!   [*Exeunt all.*

THE END.